PUBLIC POLICY IN A DIVIDED SOCIETY

Public Policy in a Divided Society

Schooling, culture and identity in Northern Ireland

ALEX McEWEN
Graduate School of Education
Queen's University, Belfast

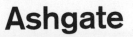

Aldershot • Brookfield USA • Singapore • Sydney

Published by
Ashgate Publishing Ltd
Gower House
Croft Road
Aldershot
Hants GU11 3HR
England

Ashgate Publishing Company
Old Post Road
Brookfield
Vermont 05036
USA

British Library Cataloguing in Publication Data
McEwen, Alex
    Public policy in a divided society : schooling, culture and
    identity in Northern Ireland
    1. Education and state - Northern Ireland 2. Education and
    state - Religious aspects - Christianity 3. Education,
    Secondary - Northern Ireland 4. Education, Secondary -
    Government policy - Northern Ireland
    I. Title
    379.4'16

Library of Congress Catalog Card Number: 98-74203

ISBN 1 84014 316 9

Printed and bound by Athenaeum Press, Ltd.,
Gateshead, Tyne & Wear.

Contents

List of Tables and Figures

Preface and Acknowledgements

A stranger visiting Northern Ireland could not help but notice the generally high level of public confidence in schools. Despite what many see as the sectarian potential of their religious segregation, parents respect teachers' efforts in trying to obtain the best academic results for their children in both sectors. For a significant and highly influential minority this means high levels of attainment with the best A level results in the United Kingdom. The underside of this pattern is the poor achievement of a substantial number of pupils on leaving school: Northern Ireland has the largest proportion of school leavers with low attainment when compared with Great Britain. Over the past 18 years, however, successive Conservative administrations in Northern Ireland have held up the schools as examples of the high standards achievable in a system that has retained grammar schools. It is only relatively recently, as the results became available, that the problem of under-achievement of a significant number of school leavers was targeted by the Department of Education for Northern Ireland (DENI) through the Raising Schools Standards Initiative. Its successor, the School Improvement Programme, reflects the change from the previous Conservative administration's approach in the new Labour government's 'third way' policy of offering rewards for schools that do well and sanctions for those that continue to under-perform. DENI has avoided the 'naming and shaming' and closure and has added the refinement of an action team to take over a failing school in order to 'turn it round'.

One of the central questions that runs through this book is why selection remains when elsewhere in the United Kingdom it has been abolished as a system-wide feature of secondary education. This is particularly so when there is evidence from Scotland, which has many similarities to Northern Ireland, that a comprehensive system can deliver real benefits on educational and social grounds. The key to understanding the reasons for holding on to selection necessarily involves an analysis of the impact of the different 'histories' of Catholics and Protestants on their cultural and political identities and the extent to which schools have been integrally bound up with the two communities' definitions of themselves as predominantly Irish or British.

The Churches have been centrally concerned with schools since they were first introduced formally by the British government in 1831 as a means of promoting better understanding between Catholics and Protestants throughout the whole of Ireland. The British administration's official policy was one of religious integration in the new National Schools. The Catholic Church was initially positive towards the reform in anticipation of the end of proselytising on the repeal in 1829 of the Penal Laws and the religious and educational privations that the laws had entailed for Catholics, Presbyterians and dissenters. The Reformation soon raised its head, however, with respect to the way religion was to be taught in the new schools: the centrality of the Bible for Protestants, especially the Presbyterians, and the intercessionary doctrine of Catholicism, placing the priest at the interpretative centre of scripture. The result of this doctrinal disagreement was that by the middle of the nineteenth century the system had become largely denominational through the control by local clergy as school managers. The religious segregation reflected another more secular dispute about the legitimacy and future governance of Ireland by Britain and the determination of Irish Nationalists to campaign for independence. A principal component of that struggle was the forging of a separate Irish identity which included the celebration of the Irish language, Gaelic sports, music and a different non-British interpretation of history. Protestants, mindful of their minority position in pre-partition Ireland, interpreted the strengthening Irish Nationalist movement as a threat to the basis of their political and economic ascendancy underpinned by the union with Great Britain. Political and cultural divergence was reflected in the National Schools which were officially integrated but became the forging grounds for the creation of separate community identities and loyalties.

After partition in 1921, the first Unionist administration made an attempt at reconciling community differences in the first Londonderry Education Act of 1923 by minimising the role of religious education in the newly formed Northern Ireland school system. The policy managed to outrage both Catholic and Protestant Churches which interpreted it as an attempt to introduce an almost wholly secular pattern of education. Subsequent amendments culminated in the 1930 Act settling a *de facto* segregated system of state schools fully funded by the government and attended predominantly by Protestants in parallel with a partially government funded voluntary sector, owned by the Catholic Church, with an almost wholly Catholic population of pupils and teachers. As Protestant political and cultural hegemony strengthened so, in an opposite direction, did Catholic attempts to create an alternative Irish and non-Unionist identity. In addition, the politically and culturally exclusory policies of successive Unionist administrations meant that, for Catholics, their schools were the chief area of public administration over which they exercised power.

The divergence of cultures and the sectarianism that is often its more perverted public representation has played a central role in educational policy in, for example, the continuation of selection and more positively the sponsorship by the government of religiously integrated schools as a means of reducing sectarianism. Selection is bound up with the two communities' political, economic and cultural aspirations: for Catholics as means of achieving equality of opportunity in the context of past discrimination and currently higher rates of unemployment than Protestants. Protestants and Catholics are similarly proud of most of the grammar school sector's excellence and the fact that their children, through the grammar schools, are able to compete on an equal footing with their counterparts in Great Britain and elsewhere despite being on the political and economic periphery of Europe. The current debate is concentrated on making the selection procedure fairer in the face of international evidence of the almost impossibility of designing a test that is culturally or socially unbiased. Discussion about the principle of selection at 11 is somewhat muted amongst parents not least because sufficient numbers can obtain grammar school places for their children: current estimates suggest that upwards of 40% of the age group are transferring to selective schools. Part of the integrated secondary schools' appeal is their comprehensive policy and the aim of attracting an all-ability intake placing the schools academically and socially, in parents' eyes, somewhere between the grammar and secondary schools. Latterly, the new Labour education minister has said publicly that he does not support selection but he recognises the majority of parents' wishes to retain the system. Their attitude reflects a familiar conundrum: they dislike the process of selection, but want their children to have a grammar school education because of the schools' added value academically, socially and in future employment opportunities.

The whole political and administrative processes of the province were turned upside down when the Stormont government was suspended in 1972. Since then Northern Ireland has been governed directly from Westminster through the Northern Ireland Office which has been responsible for all the areas of policy and government action carried out by the former devolved Stormont administration. This has become known as direct rule and has been something of a 'curate's egg' in so far as the quality of administration and government has been determined by the particular minister's knowledge of Northern Ireland's education system and enthusiasm for the post. In some cases there have been definite gains: it is arguable, for instance, that development of integrated schools would have languished if their future had been left in the hands of local politicians. The 1992-97 Conservative government's dependence on the votes of Unionist MPs delayed a long overdue reform of the top heavy administrative structure of schooling with five Education and Library Boards for a population of 1.5 million. Government proposals to reduce these and divert the money to pupils foundered on the threat by the Unionist MPs to bring down the government if the proposed plan for three Boards was put in place. In the end, however, direct rule removes local democratic control and responsibility and the 70% 'yes' vote for the Good Friday Agreement in the recent referendum will give Northern Ireland politicians their first experience of power to frame and administer educational policy as well as the other five areas of government at present under the control of the Northern Ireland Office.

The unintended effect of direct rule has been to concentrate responsibility for policy in the DENI. This has led to what McKeown (1998) has called a 'culture of officialdom' which again has had benefits and drawbacks. In maintaining continuity of policy and preserving the quality of the service DENI civil servants have performed a central role against the background of variable political appointments to education. Civil servants are nevertheless best scrutinised by local politicians who know the schools and the cultures they spring from. There are a number of references in the interviews which suggest that, whilst the DENI is not a 'secret garden' for policy-making and decisions, it sometimes appears as a private fiefdom with regard to consultation and accountability for policy. A recent example was the introduction of the national Professional Qualification for Headship through the appointment of a 'lead body' to oversee the organisation of courses leading to the qualification. In Great Britain the Department for Education and Employment (DfEE) had put this out to open tender whereas the DENI simply announced that it was to be led by the Regional Training Unit set up by the Boards to provide inservice training for teachers. Tendering looks like it will be restricted to aspects of the course's teaching rather that overall responsibility for the qualification which higher education and other institutions were able to bid for in Great Britain. More positively, the Department is attempting to improve the poor levels of achievement of pupils from schools in catchment areas of high social and economic disadvantage. The argument here is that the continuing policy of selection tends to reduce the effectiveness of its policy by emphasising further the pupils' disadvantage and already diminished academic expectations by labelling a disproportionate number of them 'failures' at 11.

The interviews with a range of those involved in educational administration and policy reveal a surprising degree of agreement between the DENI and the Local Education and Library Boards in their separate approaches to policy. It is clear, nevertheless, that the rigidity of financial control exercised by the Department leaves the Boards with little scope for innovation and renders the second tier of administration largely inert with regard to interpretation of policy. The Belfast Board's reorganisation of further education is, however, one example of a successful attempt to rationalise a proliferation of courses and resources which often duplicated each other in the former three separate colleges. The reorganisation has now gone one stage further in the establishment of the Springvale university campus, a joint enterprise between the Belfast Institute of Further and Higher Education and University of Ulster.

Many people have supported me in writing this book. Much of the original and vital groundwork was conducted by Janet Leckey in her role as the research project officer. Her summary report for the Leverhulme Trust, which provided funding for the project on which the book is based, is a remarkably clear and concise document and is constantly referred to by other researchers as well as myself. My friend and colleague Matt Salters made a vital contribution to the initial intellectual framework for the research and his ability to synthesise complex ideas and to see where they differ and the links between them never ceases to amaze me. The other member of the team Jim Paul whose knowledge of the system and the respect in which he is held enabled us to obtain a very wide range of people willing to be interviewed. Other colleagues in the Graduate School of Education have also helped by listening to and commenting on various ideas in the book and I am indebted to Tony Gallagher and Penny McKeown for their comments on sections of the manuscript. I am also indebted to Alastair Edwards for his skill in arranging the text. I should like also to thank all the interviewees for their time and patience in answering our questions.

My wife's unfailing support through the period of writing the book and especially her proof-reading of the text and arrangement of the index have been of great assistance. I should also like to thank the Leverhulme Trust for its financial support which enabled us to carry out the project. Lastly, Queen's University, in granting me leave of absence has given me the 'space' and quality thinking time to write this book. This would have been otherwise almost impossible in the pressurised environment in which academics now work.

The ideas, arguments and views expressed in the book are, however, entirely my own responsibility.

1 Historical Background to Education in Northern Ireland

Schools before and after Partition, 1921

The purpose of this chapter is to trace the historical roots of disagreement about education and their consequences for past and contemporary approaches to framing public policy with respect to schooling in Ireland. One of the first questions to be faced in tracing the background in Ireland to policy-making in education before and after partition, is where to start. The earliest point for present purposes is the period following Henry VIII's break with Rome and the subsequent decision by the Tudors to consolidate the Protestant religion in England. The consequences for Ireland were to place it in a strategically sensitive geo-political position in relation to those continental powers that remained Catholic and, in the case of Spain especially, were determined to re-establish Catholicism in England. A key principle of English foreign and ultimately domestic policy during this period was to secure the strategically vulnerable western flank of newly Protestant England from invasion by an increasingly hostile and acquisitive Catholic Europe. The practical outcome of this policy was to be the English colonisation of Ireland as a means of protecting itself from invasion.

The Normans, led by the Earl of Pembroke known as Strongbow, had earlier come to Ireland in 1170 at the invitation, ironically, of the Irish King of Leinster, Dermot McMurrough, as an ally in his struggle with the High King of Ireland Rory O'Connor, but over the following centuries they had become largely assimilated to Irish culture and language through intermarriage. They were to become part of the problem as English Kings and Queens tried to consolidate their hold on Ireland and to impose their authority on what they came to think of as their subjects. It was Queen Elizabeth I in the aftermath of the Spanish attempt to invade England in 1588, who made the most serious attempt to curb what she saw as Catholic Irish anarchy, disobedience and indifference, at best, to English interests in protecting its vulnerable western flank. Elizabeth's determination was further strengthened by the experience in 1601 of a second attempted invasion of Ireland by a Spanish fleet in alliance with an Irish land-based force led by two of the chieftains of the province of Ulster, Hugh O'Neill and his neighbour, Hugh O'Donnell. Ulster at that time was the least anglicised province of Ireland where Gaelic culture was strongest and English penetration weakest. The joint Spanish and Irish force was defeated at the battle of Kinsale which, in political terms, effectively marked the end of Gaelic Ireland and the beginning of England's determined attempt to eliminate native Irish culture, and the Catholic religion that went with it, in a country where the Protestant Reformation had not taken root. This was symbolised further by what is remembered as 'the flight of the earls' when O'Neill and O'Donnell, despite being pardoned and allowed to keep their lands after submitting and promising allegiance to the crown, were unable to countenance their effective subjugation in their own Ulster heartland. They left dramatically and secretly from Rathmullen in Co. Donegal in 1607. It was also the beginning of the synthesis between Irish Nationalism and the Catholic religion.

The solution for the Tudors and subsequent monarchs in the 17th and 18th centuries was to be the wholesale settlement of Ireland by English and Scots entrepreneurs and farmers hungry for land in what became known as the 'plantation' of Ireland. Earlier plantations had failed for lack of investment and commitment with the result that English authority was confined to the Pale, a circle of English influence of about 15 miles around Dublin. It is an irony of history that the most rebellious and Gaelic province of Ulster was also that part of Ireland where the plantation eventually took hold. This was due mostly to the influence and presence in greater and greater numbers throughout the 17th century of Scottish Presbyterian settlers who, backed by the crown, drove out the native Irish from their farms and homes. After Protestant success in the Williamite wars at the end of the 17th century in Ireland and Europe, the position of the Catholic Irish peasants was worsened when a series of laws was passed restricting their civil liberties and privileges. Among many other restrictions, the Penal Laws, enacted at beginning of the 18th century, prevented Catholics from holding any office of state, standing for parliament, and most importantly from buying land. Through the Penal Laws, schooling also became an agency of the attempted anglicisation of Irish culture through the effective proscription of Catholic schools and Catholic teachers. Sending Catholic children abroad to be educated was similarly banned. The Catholic response was the creation of a countrywide, but somewhat haphazard, system of clandestine 'hedge schools' run by former priests and Catholic scholars and teachers. They were often quite literally held in the open countryside, but out of sight from public view. A series of relief acts culminated in 1829 with the repeal of the Penal Laws. These were accompanied in 1831 by the introduction of a state-funded National System of Schools which had as a central tenet that they should be non-denominational in an attempt to rid education of the tradition, both official and unofficial, of proselytism.

The prime mover in establishing the schools was the Chief Secretary for Ireland, Edward Stanley, who wrote to the Lord Lieutenant of Ireland, the Duke of Leinster, on the need for a national system of schooling that met both Protestant and Catholic needs. The letter acknowledged what Stanley called 'unintentional proselytising'. The relevant section is worth quoting:

> The determination to enforce…the reading of Holy Scriptures without note or comment, was done with the purest of motives… it seems to have been overlooked that the principles of the Roman Catholic Church (to which, in any system intended for general diffusion throughout Ireland, the bulk of the pupils must necessarily belong) were totally at variance with this principle; and that the indiscriminate reading of the Holy Scriptures without note or comment, by children must be peculiarly obnoxious to a church which denies, even to its adults, the right of unaided private interpretation of the sacred volume with respect to articles of religious belief. (October 1831; H.C. 196)

The new National System of Schools, Stanley advised, was to be religiously integrated and administered from Dublin by a National Board of Commissioners. Educational policy was to be based on equality of treatment of religious belief which led to immediate criticism from the Church of Ireland. It was at that time the country's established Church and as such it claimed to be the only legitimate body through which education for all denominations should be organised. The Church rejected, from its position as the official Church, any provision for schooling based on religious equity. There was no support from the government for its objections which resulted in the Church of Ireland setting up its own system of schools, the Church Education Society, attendance being open to all subject to their acceptance of Bible reading as part of the curriculum. By 1860 it had created 1,700 schools attended by 80,000 pupils although its dwindling finances and the deteriorating quality of the buildings forced the Church eventually to join the National System.

The more serious and effective criticisms of the new system came from the Presbyterians who had historically been suspicious of 'popery' and objected to the integrationist ethos of the National Schools focusing on:

The mixed nature of the Board's composition, the powers retained by the Board particularly over textbooks and teachers, the separation of religious from literary instruction, the removal of the Bible as the central focus of all education and the right of clergymen of different denominations to attend the school premises for separate religious instruction. (Coolahan 1981; P.15)

Through vociferous lobbying and public protests they managed by as early as 1840 to achieve significant alterations to Stanley's original vision for the National School System. Coolahan summarises these as:

Clergymen of different faiths did not have the right to attend the school in an ex-officio capacity but they could visit as general members of the public. A separate day no longer had to be set aside for religious instruction; this could now be given at any time provided advance notice was given. Hitherto there had been an onus on the manager or teacher to exclude children of a different denomination from religious instruction other than their own. This responsibility was now changed and such children need only be excluded if their parents specifically intervened to request such exclusion. (Ibid; P.15)

Initially, the Catholic bishops supported the introduction of the National Schools as the first ostensibly integrated, non-proselytising form of schooling in Ireland. In 1838, their representative on the National Board of Commissioners, Archbishop Murray, sought the views of his fellow prelates about the progress of the new schools. He received 23 responses most of which were positive and encouraged him to continue to represent the Church's spiritual and educational interests on the Board. A few years later, however, the Catholic Bishops became increasingly critical of the textbooks authorised by the National Board, especially those which combined common secular and religious material. Their suspicions of the potential for proselytising through the Board's control of textbooks seemed to be confirmed on the publication of 'Lessons on Christian Evidence' and ' Easy Lessons on the History of Religious Worship' by Bishop Whately, the Church of Ireland's representative on the National Board. In these he alluded to Catholic worship and beliefs as having 'pagan origins'. Their response was a resolution to the Lord Lieutenant that:

No books or tracts whatsoever for the religious or moral instruction of Roman Catholic pupils, shall be admitted into a National School without the previous approbation of the four Roman Catholic Archbishops. (February 1840; Source DAA, Dublin)

Criticism of the National Schools became more muted as the Catholic and Protestant Churches were effectively allowed to go their own denominational ways with respect to religious and moral instruction as the system as a whole became increasingly dominated by the Churches through the agency of clergymen as local managers of the schools. It is worth quoting at length what the Powis Report of 1870 found with respect to how far the denominational character of the schools had proceeded:

> The most usual form (of patronship) is that of an individual minister of religion, either a Roman Catholic priest, or a Presbyterian; sometimes, but not very frequently, he is a clergyman of the Established Church…the schools are always of a *quasi* denominational character. (Para.115)

> It is greatly intensified by the situation of the school building. If the patron is a Presbyterian, he builds his school, if possible, as an adjunct to his meeting-house…So completely do the sacred and the secular buildings combine and harmonise, that it is sometimes difficult for the observer to determine which part is church, and which school. (Para.117)

> The Roman Catholic priest keeps his chapel and his school separate (and) as a rule takes far more personal interest in the religious instruction of the children, than does the Presbyterian minister. (Religious instruction) he leaves almost entirely to the teacher. The priest, however, allowing the teacher to do no more than hear the catechism…frequently gathers the children into his chapel. (Para.118)

The Report found many examples, as well, of the original ethos of the National System where schools were managed by lay patrons with mixed religion teaching staffs and pupils: 'Some lay patrons have shown themselves to be so superior to all sentiments of exclusiveness or sectarianism, as to appoint teachers of a different persuasion from that which they themselves profess'. (Ibid; Para.125). The schools suffered throughout the 19th century from government under-investment and the effects can be seen from a survey in 1902 published in the *Belfast Telegraph* (26 September, 1902). It noted that the schools, which by this time were mostly controlled by the Churches, 'Occupied the same relationship to the churches as a gentleman's stables do to his house'. In addition, the Belfast Health Commission Report of 1908 found:

> Much evidence…as to the unsatisfactory condition of Belfast schools. We ourselves visited a considerable number, and were able to satisfy ourselves that while some are quite creditable and others are good, many are very unsatisfactory indeed. Professor Lindsay quoting from personal experience, described some of them as 'filthy dens' and 'simply disgraceful' and expressed surprise that a

wealthy city like Belfast should not only permit the use of such schools, but compel the children to attend them.

The British administration of the whole of Ireland ended with partition in 1921 when negotiations between the British government and an Irish delegation culminated on the 6th of December with the signing of what was known as the Anglo-Irish Treaty. As far as the British government was concerned it had laid the foundation for a peaceful settlement of Ireland's Troubles ending, they hoped, centuries of enmity between the people of the two islands by granting the Irish autonomy over their affairs through a system of Home Rule. The successful plantation of Ulster in the 16th and 17th centuries, and in particular its most north-easterly part by Scottish and English Protestants meant, however, that the Treaty was fatally flawed in respect of the political and, always in Ireland, the religious aspirations of the plantation's descendants whose schools were an integral part of their cultural and religious separateness. Their views on future political structures in Ireland ran counter to the British government's establishment and the Irish delegation's acceptance of two Parliaments, one in Belfast representing chiefly the six counties of Antrim, Armagh, Down, Tyrone, Londonderry and Fermanagh and another in Dublin for the remaining 26 counties. Unlike the northern Protestants, the London and Dublin based parties, at the time, saw this arrangement as a temporary expedient in the process of the two Parliaments combining, sooner rather than later, and the establishment of Home Rule for the whole 32 counties of Ireland. The Treaty's full remit was suspended for one month in the six northern counties in order for them to debate whether or not they wished to be part of the new Irish Free State. The result was a foregone conclusion given the inbuilt Protestant majority of the six counties; they exercised their option of going it alone and have stayed that way ever since with the result that Ireland was partitioned into a 26 county Free State and a six county statelet which became known as Northern Ireland and which has remained part of what became the United Kingdom of Great Britain and Northern Ireland.

Schooling Reforms after Partition

The reform of education was one of the first steps taken by the new government of Northern Ireland not least because of the ragged physical state of the National Schools introduced and partially funded by the government in 1831. The scale of the task has been summarised by Farren (1995):

6

Northern Ireland inherited nothing more than the schools and colleges which had been operating within its six counties. These amounted to 2042 National Schools, 75 intermediate (post-primary mostly grammar schools), 12 model schools…Because the Boards of National and Intermediate Education had been based in Dublin, no local administration existed within Northern Ireland. The task facing the new Ministry of Education was, therefore, an enormous one. It virtually meant starting to build from the ground up…(P.38)

Administratively and politically, with respect to educational policy, the new government saw its other task as bringing the system as a whole into line with Great Britain; the start of what became a policy in most areas of government of 'step-by-step' with Westminster. The approach was in pursuit of its more general aim of creating a six county British state on the same island, but distinct and separate from, the 26 county Nationalist Free State of Ireland to the south and west. One-third of the people of the new statelet, however, disputed its legitimacy on the basis of their Irish Nationalism; that politically a unified 32 county Ireland was the best way to establish an independent and viable Irish state. From a more practical viewpoint, Catholics were acutely aware of their minority status in the newly partitioned northern part of Ireland and the economic, social, religious and cultural discrimination they were likely to suffer. The disputed legitimacy of Northern Ireland, as it became known, spilled out on to the streets precipitating two years of violent terrorism and counter-terrorism resulting in 232 deaths, the majority of whom were Catholics and substantial movements of Nationalists across the newly formed border with what became known as 'The South'. Schooling was to be the touchstone for what became a positional 'war' between Nationalists and the new and subsequent Unionist administrations which governed Northern Ireland for the first 50 years of its existence.

The new government in Belfast quickly established the Lynn Committee to investigate means of reforming the former National School system under the chairmanship of Robert Lynn, the Unionist MP for West Belfast and editor of the strongly Unionist newspaper 'The Northern Whig'. The Catholic Church refused to sit on the Committee because of its antagonism to the creation of the separate six county political and cultural entity with a built-in Protestant majority and which, it thought, along with many others, would not last for long. The Committee's first interim came out in June 1922 and was to form the basis of the Londonderry Act of 1923 which proposed a strongly secularist pattern of state-aided primary schools which was anathema to the Protestant and Catholic authorities alike.

For the Presbyterians especially, the removal of the Bible as the central focus of the education of young children during normal school hours and the prohibition of any financial support for teaching religion was something they immediately and vigorously contested. Lord Londonderry, by contrast, had framed the legislation in reference to the 1920 Government of Ireland Act which forbade either of the new governments to 'make a law so as whether directly or indirectly to establish or endow any religion'. The 1923 Education Act sought to avoid any preference for a particular denomination in schools and in this sense conformed to the spirit of the earlier Government of Ireland Act. But its religiously neutral tone was opposed by all Church representatives and an amending act was passed in 1925 which authorised local education authorities to require their schools to provide 'simple Bible instruction'. This was to be non-denominational and non-cathechistic in its teaching. Whilst the Act did not directly endow the Protestant denominations, the Catholic authorities nevertheless, interpreted the government's intention to be the provision of a broadly Protestant form of both religious and academic education in schools that accepted state funding, since simple Bible reading without any form of clerical interpretation was contrary to Catholic teaching and religious practice. It was also, they felt, antithetical to their idea of an education which was to be couched and taught in an all-embracing religious ethos.

The success of the Protestant clerics, through the political agitation of the United Education Committee of the Protestant Churches, in directly threatening the new and fragile government in alliance with the Orange Order, is an early example of the power of the Protestant Churches in establishing a state funded system of schooling which in effect endowed their religious beliefs and a more general Protestant-British ethos. This was further strengthened in the 1930 Act by effectively ensuring that only Protestant teachers would be appointed to those schools which transferred to the state through the appointment clauses of the act. These devolved authority to local school committees which recommended shortlists to the regional committee for a final decision.

By 1930, it was also clear to Protestants and Catholics alike that earlier predictions of the probable short duration of the new Northern Ireland Parliament had been incorrect. The Catholic authorities, recognising the probable permanence of the northern administration, began to temper the strictness of their policy of non-engagement with the Unionist dominated government. Whilst they adamantly refused to countenance transferring their schools into the state system because of their theological objections to simple Bible reading and what they saw as the suppression of their Irish historical

8

and cultural heritage, they nevertheless accepted partial state funding for their schools. This amounted to payment of the teachers and 50% of any new or additions to existing buildings. In total, the church received about three quarters of the costs of running their schools. The Catholic authorities were also suspicious of the newly formed local councils and their control of state funded education because of their domination by Unionist councillors. This had come about from the unrepresentative way in which local electoral boundaries had been drawn. The political imperative of securing a Unionist majority which underpinned the selection of the six counties of Northern Ireland from the original nine Ulster counties, meant that Protestant predominance at government level should also be reflected in the administration of local amenities such as housing and education. Catholic fears and suspicions were further heightened by the government's suspension in all future elections of proportional representation in 1929. This was originally included in the Anglo-Irish Treaty to ensure the proper representation of Nationalist politics in the northern Parliament.

The 1930 Education Act put denominational schooling on a statutory footing, something that had been avoided in the former National School system of the 19th century. It is important to note, however, that the state funded schools were not then nor at present officially denominational and were in fact open to all. But the statutory representation of Protestant clergy on management committees and their influence on the system's religious ethos rendered the schools unacceptable to Catholics even before any theological considerations were debated in relation to the balance of religious and secular knowledge in the curriculum. For the rest of the 20th century the majority of children, during the period of compulsory education, have attended what is effectively a segregated system of schools. The only exceptions have been the selective voluntary grammar schools and technical colleges where there had traditionally been some small degree of cross-over of Protestant and Catholic pupils. In the case of the grammar schools this depended, before 1947, on wealth and afterwards the 11+ and to some extent on wealth, since fee-paying for entrance to grammar schools for pupils 'failing' the test remained until 1989. For the technical colleges, it was related to location, that is whether or not they were in areas of predominantly Catholic or Protestant populations and that the nearest Protestant area with a college was too far away to travel. It also marked the beginning of a long stand-off between a deeply suspicious and politically and culturally antagonistic Catholic Church and a government that was at best disinterested in Catholic education whilst determined to support a state funded system influenced strongly by the Protestant transferors and

British in ethos, curriculum and organisation. For the Catholic authorities and population at large, their schools became a 'haven of self-determination', Gallagher (1993a): they represented the only major state system in their control in an otherwise hostile cultural and political environment.

Ideologically, the divergent systems became 'state apparatuses', (Althusser; 1972). For Catholics this meant the development of a 'state within a state' as the Church authorities attempted to sustain a separate Catholic identity through the creation of a network of youth organisations and guilds. For the government, the state schools embodied an ethos of Britishness as a means of sustaining a Protestant hegemony in the newly created statelet. For the Catholic Church and the Unionist Government alike, the content and process of schooling became an expression of their respective cultural and political aspirations. In Catholic schools, subjects were expressed from an all-embracing Nationalist perspective, especially in relation to history, the Irish language, music and games which were oriented towards Irish contexts and examples. The Protestant schools adopted an approach to the curriculum which assumed no difference between the children of Belfast and those of Bristol or Leeds; their needs with regard to living and working in a British culture and state were seen as identical. The 'Catholicisation' of Irish culture and history, nothing new in Ireland, became strengthened as the two systems of schooling went their culturally and educationally divergent paths.

The Government's policy of social and educational parity with England meant that the reforms set in train by the Hadow (1926) and Spens (1939) Reports would be implemented in Northern Ireland. Both of these foreshadowed greater equality of opportunity in education with respect to the statutory provision of a secondary stage of education for all children. This was to be separated from the elementary schools at the age of eleven with the introduction of what became known as the 'eleven plus', originally conceived as a test which would decide which type of secondary school children would attend according to their aptitude, as measured by intelligence tests, for an academic, practical or technical type of curriculum. Given the political and religious sensitivity of educational matters in the province, it was inevitable that the subsequent 1944 Education Act in Great Britain, introducing universal secondary education and raising the school leaving age to 15, would be framed in the light of the Churches' responses to the political debates both inside and outside parliament which led up to the legislation becoming law in 1947 in Northern Ireland. The three year delay was indicative of the natural time lag between the two areas where England normally took the lead in matters of legislation, but it also reflected the different educational contexts of Northern

Ireland, especially where reform of schooling touched on religion where criticism of the Act came from both Catholic and Protestant sources. In the former case, the Church resented and challenged the Act's intended degree of state control of schooling on the grounds that education was the responsibility of the Church in partnership with the family. The Church argued that, in guaranteeing freedom of religious conscience and worship, the state had a parallel duty to provide their material expression through funding schools based, in this case, on Catholic religious beliefs and values. It followed, the Church argued, that the government should fund Catholic schools to the same degree that it provided for schools that had transferred into the state system; in effect, state sponsored denominational schooling, something which only came about almost 50 years later. At the time, the Catholic authorities were also apprehensive of the likely burden of having to build new schools for the majority of pupils who would come into the new system of secondary intermediate schools catering for those who were thought, following the 1947 Act, to be more suited to a practical non-academic curriculum. They knew also that this would have to levied on a population already economically disadvantaged and experiencing significant levels of discrimination in employment.

The Protestant authorities were critical of what they saw as the weakening of their influence over the state schools secured in the 1930 Act, especially through the introduction of a conscience clause in the proposed Act allowing teachers to withdraw from religious teaching or worship in school on the grounds of personal beliefs or absence of them. The requirement to teach the Bible had been a condition of appointment after the 1930 provisions which the attorney general of the period leading up to the 1947 Act judged to be in contravention of the 1920 Government of Ireland Act, in that it compelled teachers who were paid from public funds to teach Bible instruction. This was generally construed by the Catholic authorities as proselytising, but more generally, it endowed a particular denomination which had been disallowed by the 1920 Act. The Protestant Churches were also opposed to the increased funding, from 50 to 65%, for Catholic schools which had not transferred into the state system but which accepted local authority members on their management committees, known as the four (owner or trustee members) and two (local authority members) schools.

The 1947 Northern Ireland Act in one sense followed in the main the tri-partite arrangements in Great Britain but, in another, were something of a travesty in terms of the somewhat less than universal provision of secondary schooling with respect to access to the selective grammar schools. With only seven of these under local authority control, the main difficulty at the time (and to the present day), was the semi-private nature of the other 64 voluntary grammar schools charged with taking the new and greatly increased enrolments of pupils successful in the test. They had managed to remain outside local authority control with owners drawn from the Catholic Church, in the case of the Catholic grammar schools, and trustees in the ostensibly secular and officially non-denominational grammar schools. In the latter, however, Protestant denominations exercised a significant residual influence although the schools continued to attract a small minority of Catholic pupils from families living in areas where there were few Catholic grammar schools available, or who rejected sectarianism. There were also families who wished to provide the most advantageous social and vocational start for their children by sending them to predominantly Protestant schools in a state where the religion of prospective employees was identified chiefly by the school they attended. This was one of the main processes through which discrimination in employment, to the disadvantage of Catholic pupils, took place.

Both types of school guarded their independence jealously and were more than reluctant to allow what they saw as interference by local and central government officials. In return for partial state funding, amounting to 65% of capital costs and a tuition cost for each child accepted, the grammar schools undertook to reserve 80% of their places for those who 'passed' the 11+ test and who were awarded what the schools managed to have defined as a scholarship. These were initially to be means tested, a condition later to be abandoned. On top of this they retained the right to charge fees. The limited space available in the grammar schools and the premium put by parents on a place, meant that the aptitude test quickly became a competition for a grammar school education limited to approximately the top 27% of the ability range.

The 1947 Act represented a significant social and educational advance through the introduction of universal secondary education formerly available only to those who could pay for it or by means of scholarships for academically able children from poor backgrounds. It followed, however, the familiar pattern of denominationalism which meant the continuation of segregation in the primary schools into the new secondary system. Catholic insistence on control of schooling meant the creation of schools for 11 to 14 year-olds (and eventually 15 year-olds) which were separate in terms of religion but at the same time unequal in relation to funding since the Catholic authorities still had to find 35% of capital costs. Initially, this level of funding was to be reserved only for those schools which accepted local authority appointees on their management committees but was extended to all voluntary schools whether or not they had 'four and two' committees. In granting this extension the government recognised that, given the amount of funds needed, a Catholic system of secondary education was, in the time span envisaged, unlikely to be built. The situation remained, however, that in effect, a significant proportion of funds had to be raised for a system-wide school building programme from an economically and politically disadvantaged community, a situation that reflected more general patterns of discrimination in employment.

The impact of the financial burden on the Catholic community was reflected in differences between rates of completion of new state and Catholic intermediate schools throughout the 1950s and 60s. At its peak in 1958/59, there were 31 more state (Protestant) than maintained (Catholic) secondary schools, a difference that was far in excess of the smaller and larger proportions of Catholic and Protestant pupils, respectively, in the wider population of the province. By 1975/76 the Catholic authorities had achieved parity largely as a result of the 1968 Education Act which brought the Catholic maintained primary and secondary schools further into the government's ambit through the Church's acceptance of joint management of their schools with the government on the basis of what was in effect the earlier 'four-and-two' pattern. The schools were to be called voluntary maintained and to be granted 85% of capital funding in addition to full funding of recurrent costs already granted on their acceptance of government representation.

The separateness of the new secondary intermediate system of schools was further underscored through the Protestant authorities' insistence on extending their rights of representation in the management of the former public elementary schools to the new intermediates. They argued that their responsibility for the pupils attending the state intermediate system was no less than those in the former elementary schools where they had been guaranteed rights with regard to the management of the schools in partnership with the state and that logic demanded it be extended to the new secondary schools. In promoting their case the Churches accused the government of bad faith and reiterated the arguments surrounding the original Lononderry Acts of the 1920s and the 1930 Act, that transferring their schools to the state meant also the continuation of the Churches' pastoral responsibility for their various 'flocks'. The local authorities agreed with their viewpoint and were willing to continue in the new intermediates the pattern of representation agreed in 1930 for the elementary schools. This view reflected the fact that local authority representation was often aligned with membership of the Protestant Churches which itself reflected the domination of local government by

Unionists. Local government acquiescence in the appointment of Protestant transferors was interpreted by the Protestant Churches as something less than the statutory right of representation they sought. The White Paper of 1964, after prolonged lobbying and argument with the Unionist government, granted the extension. Enrolments for that year show the almost total segregation of schooling along denominational lines: 51.2% attended the predominantly Protestant state sector whilst 48.8% were in the predominantly Catholic schools, a 'cross-over' rate of 2.4%, that is, where pupils went to a school outside their actual or nominal religious denomination.

On the surface, it appears that the main policy dynamic in education in the 19th and 20th centuries has been denominationalism with the practical outcome of a system of schooling underpinned by an all-pervading ethic of separateness according to religious belief. This ran counter to the government's official policy in the 19th century of religious integration, a position initially supported by the Catholic Church which welcomed the official ending of proseltyism and antipathy towards Catholicism and seemed to the Catholic authorities to follow logically on from their emancipation in 1829. The government's policy was frustrated early on by the insistence on the part of the Protestant Churches that the Bible had to be an integral part of teaching. This was especially so in the case of the politically more important Presbyterians who objected strongly to the separation of religious and secular instruction, a practice that was integral to the rules governing teaching in the National Schools. The religious, and by extension educational disagreements, between the Protestant and Catholic Churches have their roots in the Reformation with respect to the Churches' different views about the role of individual conscience in reading and interpreting Scripture. The practical result was the creation by the middle of the century of a National System of schooling which was for the most part denominational in character in so far as they were managed by clergymen or their representatives. The chief exception to this pattern were the factory schools mostly created as result of the 1844 Factory Acts which regularised the working conditions of children who worked in the mills. The children were known as 'half-timers' and were permitted to work half of the day in the mill on condition that they attended school for the other half. Most of these schools remained integrated along the lines of the original intentions of the Stanley letter and the rules of the National System and where they still exist, remain so. The requirement of a certificate of attendance at the factory schools had the effect of securing a modest education, at least, for the 'half timers' most of whom would not have attended school at all before the introduction of the 1844 Factory Acts.

The piece-meal acceptance of denominationalism by the government in the 19th century and its more public and defining aspect of schooling in the 20th, reflect a deeper struggle for power between the two groups. In the case of Protestants, control of education was and remains a central element of an ideology of separateness formed in the context of their original position as 'planters' and in order to distinguish them from the native Celtic Irish. Schooling was introduced coercively as part of the colonisation of Ireland and, in common with all ruling classes, the original Protestants had to present their values and interests as superior to those held by the native Catholic Irish, whom they had dispossessed. It was one of the chief means of legitimising their economic, political and cultural dominance with the ultimate aim to replace force as the chief method of sustaining compliance. Over time, this ideological imperative becomes presented in colonised countries as the ideal or universally valid form of cultural reproduction,

The creation by the British administration of a National System of schools was an acceptance of the failure of coercion as represented chiefly, but not exclusively, by the Penal Laws. It was also the attempt to introduce an ideology of assimilation. The government took the view that in educating Catholic and Protestant children together through an integrated system of schooling, friendships would be formed that would outlive formal schooling and, more generally, that through close association in the classroom and playground pupils would learn about and come to understand their counterpart's viewpoints and aspirations whether Catholic or Protestant. It failed in this primary purpose ostensibly because of initial Protestant opposition to separating secular and religious education especially in the centrality, for Presbyterians, of Bible reading in children's education. Whilst the Catholic authorities were equally doubtful about the distinction between religious and secular education, they were willing, at the outset, to set these aside in the belief that the National Schools signalled the end of government hostility not only to their religion, but also its expression and practice in the classroom. As the original rules for the teaching of religion were altered in the face of Protestant objections, the 19th century National System began, for Catholics, to resemble only a weakly attenuated form of proselytising.

The disputes over the nature and direction of education in the National Schools, which developed into an organising principle of separateness for both Catholic and Protestant Churches in the running of their schools, accompanied a more fundamental power struggle over ownership of land. Agitation for land reform provided the essential driving force for a more radical political ideology of separateness in the government of Ireland; that Home

15

Rule should be the future means for the Irish to govern themselves. Education became part of this wider political campaign for independence in the extent to which Protestant and Catholic control of schools, and the different emphases given to aspects of the curriculum, especially history and the Irish language, were expressions of increasingly divergent cultural identities. These have often been characterised as Irishness and Britishness in terms of the historical and cultural capital on which the Catholic and Protestant communities drew in defining themselves. Their different identities largely determined attitudes towards each other's religious beliefs and towards their respective political aspirations. During the volatile period of the late 19th and early 20th centuries leading up to partition in 1921, suspicion and mistrust towards the 'other side' were shaped and intensified by the cleavage imposed by definitions of themselves in terms of political and cultural Nationalism and Unionism that influenced almost every educational, cultural and political issue of the day.

After partition, integration was attempted briefly by Lord Londonderry, the first minister of education in the new Unionist government in his 1923 Education Act, but amendments in 1925 and especially 1930, institutionalised formally the denominational cleavage of schooling that had grown up in the 19th century. Antagonism between the Churches and the newly formed Ministry of Education continued for most of the 20th century although by 1992 the Catholic Church felt able to accept 100% funding for capital and recurrent costs of its voluntary maintained schools, representing a historically significant rapprochement between the Catholic Church and the state. The acceptance by the Church of full state funding for its schools was conditional on them continuing to reflect a Catholic ethos. In practice, this means that the role of clergy will be unchanged and the teaching force will remain predominantly Catholic, especially in the primary schools where pupils are prepared for first communion.

A number of policies have come together in enabling the Catholic Authorities, on the one hand, to accept what is, in effect, a state-funded voluntary system and, on the other, for the government to subvent schools which they do not own and for the Church, ostensibly, to retain a significant degree of autonomy over the management and ethos of the system. Firstly, the introduction of a Northern Ireland Curriculum, similar in the main to the National Curriculum in England and Wales, means that there are no curricular differences between schools accepting state funding; past diversity in approaches by Catholic and Protestant schools to subjects such as history and to some extent music are now negligible. Secondly, the Council for Catholic Maintained Schools, established in 1987, operates, in regard to appointments of staff and curricular matters, in a similar way to the province's Education and Library Boards (Local Education Authorities in Great Britain). This was an improvement on the former position where many Catholic schools had similar responsibilities as an individual Education Board, a position borne in on them when pupil numbers began to drop in the 1980s and teachers had either to be transferred or made redundant. The Local Education Boards set up a Trawl Scheme for re-deploying redundant teachers in schools within their control which had vacancies, whilst the Catholic Schools, sympathetic as they were to the plight of redundant teachers, had no mechanism to set up a system-wide re-deployment scheme. Thirdly, the Catholic Authorities have in general been more positive to direct rule from Westminster after the suspension of the former Northern Ireland Government in 1972. The Church's attitude towards the government and its Department of Education arises from its approval of a wider pattern of policies aimed at redressing the causes of discrimination, intentional or otherwise, built up over the previous 50 years of one-party government. The most telling feature, in terms of its consequences, was in the different types of employment, in terms of status and pay, held by Protestants and Catholics and its converse, their contrasting experiences of unemployment. In both respects Catholics were at a disadvantage.

The Fair Employment Agency (now Commission) set up in 1976, is one example of the effects of direct rule in combating what is a historic pattern of disadvantage of employment. The Commission has regularised the ways in which jobs are advertised, the conduct of interviews, the requirement of neutral, that is, non-sectarian work environments and the statutory responsibility of firms with more than 11 employees to monitor and report to the Commission the denominational balance of their workforce. The Commission's policy is for firms to reflect the religious balance of the their neighbourhoods in the workforce. The Commission acknowledges the difficulty of its task in the close-knit community of Northern Ireland where, because of its peripheral economic position in relation to markets and manufacturing base, rates of unemployment have remained high:

> The informal networks which are still so powerful in Northern Ireland and through which so much employment is found, operate to maintain and reinforce employment patterns already established. Once these patterns have been established such a method of filling jobs means that, even if there were never in Northern Ireland a single instance of individual discrimination in the future, the pattern laid down will remain much the same. (Murray and Darby 1980; P.5)

17

In the context of education, the Commission's rules apply to the appointment of schools' ancillary staff, caretakers, cleaners and so on, but not to teachers, presumably because of the need to employ communicant members of the Church in order to sustain a Catholic ethos or spirit as is the case with Church schools in Great Britain. Direct rule has also resulted in greater cultural equality in the public representation of Irishness in broadcasting where the BBC currently has Irish medium programmes and others concentrating on learning the language. There are also a number of Irish medium schools receiving government funding. In addition, schools are required to create programmes of Education for Mutual Understanding (EMU) and Cultural Heritage, as part of the Northern Ireland Curriculum, whose aim is to reduce sectarian suspicion and mistrust by teaching, in the context of normal curricular subjects, relevant aspects of Nationalist and Unionist culture to Protestant and Catholic pupils alike. As part of the Education Reform Order in 1989, the equivalent of the 1988 Education Reform Act in England and Wales, the government is also now committed to supporting the growth of integrated education. This policy, similar to the National System of the 19th century, involves the establishment of new religiously integrated schools or a change in status of an existing school to become, either an integrated state or maintained integrated school. In all cases the schools must aim at a balance of pupils and staff, in the proportion of 60:40 according to either religious denomination, but not less than 30% of the smaller religious denomination.

The Protestant Churches, having secured what they felt to be sufficient influence in the direction and ethos of the state schools, have concerned themselves largely with everyday educational matters, only lately revisiting the arguments surrounding the Churches' rights and duties as transferors of their schools raised originally in the earlier part of the century. The Protestant Churches feel that their role in maintaining their individual denominational voices in the management of the state schools has been diminished when compared to what they see as the generous treatment of the Catholic Authorities as the 1989 Reform has unfolded. Since 1987 there has been a Council for Catholic Maintained Schools which has been given oversight of the Church's schools in relation to staffing and curriculum advice. The Protestant Churches are currently campaigning for a similar council to represent their values and religious interests in the same way that the Catholic Church's schools are managed by the recently created Council for Catholic Maintained Schools:

> The erosion of the Education and Library Boards' powers which was finalised by the ERO (Education Reform Order for Northern Ireland, 1989) has in turn reduced the influence of transferor representatives at that level. This was

occurring at the same time as the DENI was enabling and funding the establishment of a Council for Catholic Maintained School and enhancing the integrated option which now has a similar 'quango' in the Northern Ireland Council for Integrated Education. Basically, the time is overdue for a body to provide a similar focus for the controlled (Protestant) schools. (McKelvey 1993; P.77)

The much used or abused instrument of convenience the Government of Ireland Act of 1920 is once more invoked to strengthen the case:

There is a consensus of opinion on the three Churches' Boards that in this area the government may be acting in a discriminatory fashion contrary to the terms of the Government of Ireland Act, 1920. (Ibid; P. 77)

It could be argued, however, that a very strict interpretation of the Act could lead to the view that the funding of schools endowing a particular religion, in the case of the Catholic system, and the special position and influence of the Protestant clergy in the state schools, were both in contravention of the Act, (Akenson; 1973). This interpretation of the 1920 Government of Ireland Act, if it has ever been officially considered since the 1930 Education Act, has always been superseded in the view of the Catholic Church by the importance placed on the doctrinal role of the school in educating Children in the faith: that to deny the Church freedom in educating its children would be a contradiction of the right to practice the religion itself. This is a view that was been accepted by successive Unionist administrations.

Lastly, both sets of schools, whilst remaining religiously segregated, have been influenced by the government's policies on accountability with regard to publishing their examination results, truancy rates and, in the primary sector, parents' knowledge about their rates of 11+ 'successes'. This has led to a more general concern with what has been called 'credentialism' as expressed in higher qualifications required to gain employment than in the past. Schools, as a consequence, are now under great pressure to produce better GCSE and A Level results, as well as numbers of pupils gaining entrance to higher and further education. The effects on Catholic schools with respect to the transmission of a specifically religious ethos and practice have been noted by O'Boyle (1993) who carried out research on two schools, a boys' and a girls' single-sex school, where, in pushing for higher grades, the religious mission of the schools had become formulaic. He quotes an interview with a school chaplain:

Now you talk about Catholic schools having a Catholic ethos, but that's not true, a lot of Catholic Schools don't have a Catholic ethos, they have an academic ethos, or a sporting ethos. It comes through, 'how much time or disruption are you prepared to allow things to happen'? Take the boys' grammar: it's almost impossible to work in from a time point of view because there's so much pressure on academically, the chaplain is on the periphery. There's much more freedom in the boys' secondary (non-selective) school. For example, I would take fifth year groups for discussions, say at PE time. That would be an impossibility in the grammar school…for mass there's no preparation. It becomes the same as Sunday Mass. (P. 201)

Conclusion

Throughout the 19th and 20th centuries successive governments have been faced with the problem of managing an educational system in a society where political, cultural and economic stability is undermined by the faultline of opposing identities. These have affected the ways in which Protestants and Catholics define themselves with respect to most aspects of their lives. In the 19th century, the then British administration was able to create an integrated pattern of schooling throughout the whole of Ireland in the belief that educating children together would be a powerful means of reducing community-based prejudices about each other. A similar attempt is currently underway with approximately 3% of the province's pupils attending religiously integrated schools supported by the Department of Education for Northern Ireland. Whilst the overall numbers of pupils in what is now called the integrated sector is low, the rate of growth has been impressive starting with twenty eight pupils in a scout hall in 1981, to a projected enrolment in 1998 of approximately eleven thousand.

The policy of non-denominational schooling was effectively frustrated during the 19th century because of the Churches' attitudes towards the government's wider political and cultural intentions and policies. The Churches also mistrusted each other's motives and guarded jealously their grip on clerical power in addition to their control of schooling, as it either promoted or diminished the pursuit of the economic and political interests of their respective communities. This was repeated in the period immediately after partition in 1921 as the denominationally neutral Londonderry Act of 1923 became in 1930 the blueprint for a government sanctioned system of schools segregated according to religion, either Protestant or Catholic, for the greater mass of children. The Catholic Church's refusal to transfer its schools into the state system, whilst it was based on the grounds of religious conscience and doctrine, was to have far reaching effects in terms of the impoverishment of the educational provision that the Church, with only partial government funding, was able to offer. The Standing Advisory Commission for Human Rights Report of 1992 'The Financing of Schools in Northern Ireland' suggested a further hidden under-funding of Catholic schools. Informal estimates put this at about £20,000,000 when compared to the state sector over this period of time (Cormack et al; 1992).

One conclusion that has been drawn from the Report suggests that Catholic pupils have been disadvantaged in their opportunity to take up science subjects because of the relative sparseness of high cost laboratories and a consequent shortage of qualified teachers. This has also contributed to the employment prospects of Catholic pupils, the argument goes, who still remain twice as likely to be unemployed as their Protestant counterparts with similar qualifications. Murrray (1993) puts the two sides of the issue:

> ...if it could be demonstrated that Catholic schools have suffered as a result of differential and unfair funding, to the extent that curriculum provision or resources have been affected, then it can be claimed that the Department of Education and the Education and Library Boards have infringed the rights of pupils in Catholic schools. If on the other hand it can be shown that curricular emphases *(and bias towards arts subjects)* existing in Catholic schools are a consequence of a deliberate choice on the part of those schools, and if children suffer on the job market as a result then a similar accusation can be made against the schools themselves. (P.209-210) *Original author's italics.

As the curriculum, funding and management of the two sets of schools are now almost identical following the 1989 reforms, it would be tempting to speculate that they would begin to co-operate more closely on the grounds of recognising their similar interests in, for example, contesting government polices where they ran counter to the schools' mutual interests or acting jointly in order to influence policy. Such a development would be subject, however, to the resolution of the larger question of identity since the Protestant and Catholic Churches' outwardly denominational interests in schooling represent deeper political and cultural questions posed by their respective communities. In this respect O'Dowd (1989) argues that the Catholic Bishops were effectively the main political opposition for a large part of the period before 1972 when the former National Party had a policy of abstentionism and refused to be the official opposition: 'It was the Catholic Church, rather than the various political groupings which typically represented Northern Nationalists in their dealings with the Unionist state' (P.119).

This is especially so in the retention of their respective schools with the government's policy towards them taken as a touchstone for its treatment of the two communities' wider cultural and political ambitions. These have been pursued through the ballot box by the broad mass of the Catholic community, but also by recourse to the bomb and bullet by a small violent minority. They concern the political legitimacy of the state and its ability to guarantee equity of opportunity in employment and recognition of political and cultural Nationalism. The Protestant community, in turn, feels itself undermined by the British government's view that it has no 'selfish economic or political interest' in staying in Northern Ireland and in conjunction with other political developments since then, including The Anglo-Irish Agreement of 1985 and The Framework Document of 1993, sees itself as a community being propelled towards minority status within a 32 county united Ireland. In electoral terms, it has expressed strong support for political and economic union with Great Britain whilst a small minority has pursued more violent means of promoting political Unionism. Until some accommodation is achieved between these questions of identity, separate schooling remains one of the chief ways in which Protestants and Catholics wish to sustain their differing definitions of themselves and as a means of projecting the underlying cultural and political patterns of, on the one hand, a separate Northern Ireland state and on the other, a new form of political arrangement involving closer political, cultural and economic relationships with the other 26 counties of Ireland and bringing to an end the British presence in Ireland.

2 Schooling and Identity

Separate Schools: Separate Identities

The central argument in chapter one and indeed throughout this book is that public policy in education is framed against the background of disagreement among Protestants and Catholics about their deep-rooted cultural and political identities. Religious denomination and segregated schooling are the outward signs of an underlying dispute concerning, from a Nationalist viewpoint, the legitimacy of the state itself and for Protestants a way of securing the Union through the state schools' ethos of cultural and educational Britishness. Additionally, a separate denominational school system represents Catholics' right to express freedom of worship through schooling as a principle superseding any perceived consequences of the sort of social and cultural 'apartheid' that many now feel is sustained by denominational schooling. This is not to ignore other important aspects of the conflict which an early analysis set out in the Cameron Report of 1969. It noted, in addition to mistrust and suspicion over denominational schooling, a number of grievances affecting mainly the Catholic population: housing allocation, discrimination in employment, gerrymandering of election boundaries, the actions of the 'B' Specials (a predominantly Protestant auxiliary police force), the Special Powers Act - later used to bring in detention without trial - and failure to obtain recompense for complaints.

Protestant fears, according to Cameron, were expressed chiefly in the context of what they saw as increasing powers ceded to the Nationalist community by the 'appeasing' O'Neill government of the 1960s. This was in addition to the perceived threat of being 'bred out' by a higher Catholic birth rate leading, it was feared, to a united Ireland by demography rather than politics. Whilst these grievances were common currency within the two communities, the Cameron Report, issued after the first outbreak of the present phase of the Troubles, was nevertheless the first government inspired and authoritative statement of the cultural, social, educational and political faultlines that ran through Northern Ireland and which rendered it somewhat less than a civil society. The Report was also notable for its concentration on what Whyte (1990) calls 'internal conflict' type of explanations:

> The Cameron Report represents the high-water mark of the internal-conflict interpretation. It was the product of the special circumstances of 1968-69, when the civil rights movement, far from raising wider questions of national allegiance, was simply claiming British rights for British citizens. (P. 195)

> The internal-conflict interpretation, though it has become by far the most popular, suffers, like the other interpretations, from difficulties. The drawback of the traditional Nationalist school is that it took insufficient account of the separate identity of northern Protestants. The drawback of the traditional Unionist school is that it took insufficient account of the community divide within Northern Ireland. A limitation of the internal-conflict school is that, though there is agreement in broad terms on the nature of the problem, there is no agreement on the nature of the solution. (P.205)

Previous Nationalist and Unionist explanations of the conflict, Whyte argues, in both all-Ireland and Northern contexts, had tended to see the causes of the problem as 'exogenous'. In its most direct Nationalist form, this viewpoint argues that the British presence in Ireland had led not only to the suppression of Irish nationality, but also prevented Protestants from seeing what they had in common with their Catholic neighbours and the benefits, they argued, that a united Ireland would bring. The logical conclusion of this ideology was the removal of the British and the creation of an independent Ireland in which Protestants participated as equals. Unionists' thinking went in the opposite direction: that the maintenance of the union was the only way to secure their position as a threatened minority in an all-Ireland context and, conversely, the need to create and sustain a Protestant hegemony within the six counties of Northern Ireland. The re-organisation of education in both parts of Ireland after partition reflected these opposing ideologies of Irish nationality. In the new 26 county Free State an early prominent sign of the southern authorities' approach to the creation of an Irish identity through schooling was the adoption of a policy of gaelicisation affecting teachers and pupils alike:

> Gaelicisation included the requirement that teachers and student-teachers attend special summer courses in Irish and the reform of the curriculum in the training colleges to take account of developments at primary school level...the author's suggestions for English indicated a bias against those of British nationality,...it was decided that students answering examination questions in Irish would qualify for bonus marks on a sliding scale from 10% downwards. (Farren 1995; P.111)

The Catholic Church's role in framing policy was strengthened and it became more generally the new Free State's chief moral arbiter occupying a central position in decisions to ban 'evil' literature, films and other 'unsuitable' cultural forms with legislation following in 1929 for the censorship of literature and to control public dancing in 1935.

Such initial zeal in implementing a strongly gaelicised concept of Irishness in reforming education in southern Ireland might have been expected in the first initial enthusiasm for independence in order to distinguish it from the British initiated National Schools. It proved discomfiting, however, for southern Protestants who felt sufficiently threatened to seek assurances of their continuing place in the new state. One feature which they took exception to was what they called the Catholicisation of Irish language textbooks. They were given assurances by the new Minister of Education, Eoin MacNeill who deferred to Protestant sensitivities by modifying the Irish language programme for students in the Church of Ireland teacher training colleges. For northern Protestants it looked positively alienating and strengthened the new administration's policy of synchronising Northern Ireland's schools with those in Britain in order to ensure, through schooling, what the new prime minister, James Craig, called 'a Protestant state for a Protestant people'. More practically, it ensured that the province's pupils and their qualifications were recognised in Great Britain and that they were able to compete on level terms with children in Scotland, England and Wales for jobs and higher education places.

In framing educational policy through what became known as a 'step-by-step' reflection of the system in England and Wales, with suitable local amendments, the northern Unionist government was following a similar 'exogenous' ideology to the southern government, but one with a different direction in that the Unionist government was determined to minimise Irishness in the curriculum and in the cultural and political ethos of the new school system. By contrast, the Catholic Church, through its schools, fostered an ethos that fused religious and cultural beliefs and knowledge. This policy represented a means of both preserving its doctrinal autonomy and an alternative identity for its people clearly separated from the government-inspired Britishness of the state schools. The Catholic authorities saw their schools as a way of creating a legitimate foundation for the preservation of an Irish educational culture in what they perceived to be a hostile northern political and cultural climate.

The Dual System of Schooling

Schooling in Northern over the period since partition has developed into a two track system according to religious denomination: effectively this has meant pupils attending predominantly Protestant or Catholic schools. Politically, Nationalist dissatisfaction with the 1921 settlement and the Catholic community's experience of discrimination in housing and employment rendered education as the only major area of public life and employment over which they exercised power. It became the focus for judging successive governments' treatment of Catholics' wider and political identities and cultural aspirations. These were often translated into disputes over the number of representatives nominated by the Church, the local authority and the government on school management committees. Protestant authorities were equally vigilant in their scrutiny of government policy towards education seeing their schools as an essential element of sustaining their separate culture and ultimately its political expression through the preservation of the union. Broadly speaking, the dual system of schools developed among their respective populations a sense of Britishness for Protestant pupils and Irishness for Catholic pupils. State schools in Northern Ireland, whilst officially non-denominational and culturally neutral, have historically been perceived by Protestant and Catholics alike as predominantly Protestant in ethos and orientation. Politically, they have been seen as supportive of Unionist values and culturally as an important source for the creation and transmission of a British cultural and political identity. As a consequence, Catholic parents have been reluctant to send their children to state schools since the state has been synonymous with values and policies which, after partition, increasingly marginalised their economic, political and cultural interests.

Alongside the state or in Northern Ireland controlled schools (by the Educational and Library Boards which are similar to the Local Education Authorities in Great Britain) is a parallel structure of schools owned by the Catholic Church Authorities and administered by the Council for Catholic Maintained Schools (CCMS). As far as the curriculum is concerned, the Catholic schools are almost the same as the state schools with the defining difference that teaching is conducted against an all embracing religious ethos. Outwardly the difference between the two types of school can be seen in the sports that pupils are taught: Gaelic football is played in Catholic schools only. Soccer would be played in both schools whilst rugby would be confined almost wholly to the Protestant selective grammar schools and some state secondaries. Many of the Catholic schools would also display religious paintings and statues. Some, although by no means all, state schools would, by contrast, have pictures of the Queen or other members of the Royal Family in public areas of the school and would also display the Union flag on the Queen's birthday or other similar official 'state' days, usually near the entrance to the school. Murray (1988) gives some interesting insights into Protestant and Catholic teachers' perceptions of these symbols and prejudices towards them when visiting each other's school. Both sets of teachers found them at best culturally and religiously alien.

With the exception of a small religiously integrated sector, (about 3% of the school population) primary and post-primary schools can for all practical purposes be described as Protestant or Catholic in outlook and ethos. The Catholic grammar schools are owned by the Church and the Protestant grammar schools by trustees, both types of school administer their own affairs outside the control of the local Education and Library Boards or the Council for Catholic Maintained Schools, dealing directly with the Department of Education. Some degree of transfer between the various types of school does occur where mostly Catholic parents choose to send their children to Protestant grammar schools rather than to a similarly selective Catholic school. In 1994, for example, in the Belfast Board area 150 (6.7%) children transferred out of the Catholic school system of whom 79 obtained the highest grades A and B in the transfer procedure (the 11+ test). These pupils went to Protestant grammar schools which would also have attracted Catholic and Protestant pupils from outside the Belfast Board area. In the South Eastern Board area, 89 (5.6%) Catholic pupils transferred out the Catholic schools, 49 (3.1%) to integrated secondary schools and 40 (2.4%) to Protestant grammar schools: of these 37 had obtained a grade A in the 11+ (McCavera 1997).

Such transfers may be accounted for by geographical or demographic factors where there are insufficient numbers of pupils of either denomination to support separate schools. In the past it was also a means of improving Catholic children's economic life chances in the face of entrenched forms of discrimination. The first identifying feature of this informal but powerful selection process was often the school which a prospective employee attended. The figures suggest, however, that a significant proportion of Catholic parents with high ability children are choosing to send their children to Protestant grammar schools. The explanation for this apparent cross-over effect may lie in more general social changes brought about by the outcomes of past educational policies in the promotion of educational opportunity through, for example, the 1947 Act, and the employment legislation enacted since 1972 outlawing employment discrimination on the grounds of religion and gender.

These measures have resulted in the growth of a confident and self-aware Catholic upper middle class, a small proportion of whom appear to see the Protestant grammar schools as the best means of ensuring a similar social and occupational outcome for their children.

Culture and Identity: The Impact on Education Policy

To explain the dual system of schooling in the province in purely religious terms would be both misleading and incomplete because of the schools' pivotal role in the protection of the two communities' traditions and cultures. In the past, this feature of schooling was most obvious in the schools' differing emphasis in the teaching of history, teaching the Irish language, some aspects of music and choice of sports. Until recently, for example, 19th and 20th Irish history, especially the development of Irish Nationalism, was simply not taught in most Protestant post-primary schools. Protestants attending the state schools, for example during the 1940s and 50s, were taught British and European history in much the same way as pupils in Leeds or Bristol on the assumption, largely taken for granted in the Protestant community, that the history of Irish Nationalism was not only irrelevant for British pupils in Northern Ireland, but potentially subversive. It is still the case even within the same, now statutory history curriculum, that there could be differences of emphasis according to the particular ethos of the school or the views of individual teachers.

One of the aims of recent government policy has been to enhance those aspects of their respective traditions which Protestant and Catholic pupils share and respect for those on which they differ. As part of the curriculum reforms, for example, schools are now required to teach the two cross-curricular themes of education for mutual understanding and cultural heritage. All pupils must now take these in the context of their normal curricular subjects with the aim of redressing the balance of sectarian myth concerning 'the other side' and the sort of distorted history which accompanies them. The cross curricular themes, designed to reduce Protestant and Catholic distrust and prejudice towards each other's cultural and political identities, are the practical outcome of a shift to what Whyte (1990) calls an 'endogenous' or internal conflict explanation of Northern Ireland's Troubles. While recognising the role of the Westminster and Dublin governments in framing and funding policy, the argument, he suggests, shifts towards the differing and antagonistic ways in which the two communities regard and relate to the two 'outside' administrations. Catholic experience of Unionist governments has been one of exclusion of power and the subsequent political and civic abuses that developed and given at least passive support by Westminster. Protestants, by contrast, enjoyed a 50 year hegemony in all aspects of the political and cultural life of Northern Ireland with the exception of control over Catholic schooling.

Successive administrations were willing to cede control of the Catholic schools to the Church on the grounds both of freedom of conscience and the fact that this was balanced by the significant level of influence of Protestant clergy in the state schools. More recently, the Westminster government in recognition of the unsatisfactory outcome of partition and Nationalist aspirations and the inherent political instability of the province, has rendered the union conditional in so far as its continuation will depend on a majority vote of the people of Northern Ireland. Such an unusual step, in international terms, of offering up part of its territory on the outcome of a plebiscite, undermines the political position of Protestants whilst also, they argue, giving indirect support to the 'armed struggle' by republicans to remove the British presence by force. Conversely, Protestant paramilitaries use force to support the union. It is inevitable in such an unstable political milieu that educational policy will become another aspect of the internal conflict over the future shape of Northern Ireland. In this respect it reflects both an attempt at, and the difficulties of, promoting some degree of basic social and cultural consensus. In this it is seriously compromised by the sheer weight of separation of children in their schooling according to religion. Research on schools in the province suggests that attempts to promote greater cross-community understanding through, for example the cross curricular themes or exchange visits between the two types of school, are undermined by the structure of segregated denominational schools. Darby (1987) and Greer and Long (1989) show that schools are an important arena for the communication of sectarian ideas and myths for pupils. In building up a sense of identity the research emphasises the significance for both sets of pupils of a hidden curriculum of sectarian attitudes outside the classroom. These are often distorted accounts of a community's history and traditions connected with, for example, the establishment of the Protestant ascendancy after the Williamite Wars of the 17th century or, alternatively, the commemoration of the republican uprising of Easter 1916.

Curriculum Policy and the Politics of Identity

In combating the different types of sectarian distortions of history and culture, the government through the 1989 Education Reform Order, (the Northern Ireland version of the National Curriculum in England and Wales), took a strongly pro-active approach to achieving a better understanding by each community of the other's history and culture. Two programmes have been devised: cultural heritage and education for mutual understanding which are to be taught to all pupils in the context of all the more usual curricular subjects with the greatest officially determined weighting going to areas such as English and history. Along with the cross curricular theme of education for mutual understanding, it is meant to bring about a greater appreciation by Protestants and Catholics of each other's cultural, political and historical traditions and in the long term to remove the causes of present community mistrust and animosity. Teachers must incorporate the cross curricular themes in the normal curricular subjects of history, English, geography, science and so on, and they are required to include the scheme's objectives in their syllabuses.

The problems which the cross curricular programmes attempt to confront can be encapsulated neatly in two alternative analyses of the causes of community conflict and mistrust. The first places the emphasis on schooling and the extent to which it may have contributed to the present Troubles through the educational, social and cultural segregation of Catholic and Protestant children in their respective school systems. This analysis has been the organising principle behind the establishment and growth of religiously integrated schools where Catholic and Protestant children are taught together. The schools are organised on the basis of having an agreed balance of the two religious groups in order to avoid one particular viewpoint or ethos becoming dominant.

The alternative viewpoint places more emphasis on economic and political factors as having fostered suspicion, mistrust and discrimination. Many have argued that this provides a more likely and more powerful basis for explaining present levels of inter-community tension. Proponents of the latter analysis would point especially to patterns of employment which result in different levels and quality of opportunity being presented to Catholics and Protestants as a significant strand of the bitterness and distrust that has grown up in each community, especially since partition and the unchallenged political ascendancy of successive Unionist governments in which discrimination in employment became widespread. Aunger (1981) suggests that:

While a clerk may be a Catholic, it is more likely that the office manager will be a Protestant; while a skilled craftsman may be a Catholic, it is more likely that the supervisor will be a Protestant; and while a nurse may be a Catholic, it is more likely that the doctor will be a Protestant. (P.8)

He also shows from census figures that Protestants were over-represented in the three highest classes, whilst proportionally more Catholics were at the lower end. Catholics were also working in industries with less security of employment and lower pay such as construction and other lower status service jobs. Protestants on the other hand, were more often employed in higher paid and skilled industries like engineering, and in more senior posts in government employment such as the civil service and other public employment. The effect Aunger argues was 'a noteworthy congruence between the class cleavage and the religious cleavage in Northern Ireland' (P. 17). Whyte (1990) argues that the employment and class differentials between Protestants and Catholics, to the disadvantage of the latter, go a considerable way towards explaining community distrust and disharmony:

It is worth dwelling on Northern Ireland's poor economic situation because it helps to explain the community division. If the region were prosperous, one might expect prosperity to alleviate community tensions...But in Northern Ireland, two communities are scrambling for inadequate resources. Catholics on average are worse off than Protestants on average, but it is not easy to improve the lot of Catholics without damaging that of Protestants. (P. 53)

Despite the introduction of fair employment legislation during the period of direct rule, young Catholics are approximately twice as likely to be unemployed as Protestants. Current figures from the Standing Commission for Human Rights inquiry into employability suggest that the pattern has not changed over the period of 25 years since the Cameron report of 1974 (McGill; 1997). The figures have been criticised, by Breen and Gudgin (1996), however, on the grounds that insufficient weight is given to different demographic patterns in the Protestant and Catholic communities. They argue simply that the higher birth rate within Catholic families would necessitate the creation of increasing numbers of jobs to keep abreast of the proportionately higher levels of Catholic school leavers coming on to the labour market. They also point out that the same pattern of Protestant advantage in employment exists in southern Ireland related, they argue, more to social class and educational effects than any sectarian bias in the opportunity structure:

Second, these results suggest that the common practice of deducing from a high unemployment ratio (between 2.0 and 2.5 in favour of Protestants) that discrimination *must* be a cause is quite wrong. If it is the case that there is little *systematic* discrimination in Northern Ireland then any Act aimed at reducing the unemployment ratio by combating systematic discrimination is unlikely to succeed unless it was unintentionally to introduce an element of discrimination against Protestants into the labour market. A more effective means of reducing the unemployment ratio than legislation is in our view to reduce the numbers unemployed rather than attempting to switch unemployment from one community to another…Any measure which succeeded in halving unemployment in this way (Action for Community Employment Scheme) would reduce Catholic: Protestant unemployment ratio to around 1.6. At this level the ratio would be only a little higher than that between Presbyterians and Church of Ireland members in Northern Ireland, and would be lower than the Catholic: Protestant unemployment ratio in the Republic of Ireland (Gudgin and Breen; 1996, P. 42-43). *Original author's italics.

The Gudgin and Breen paper contains critical reviews of their work by other economists suggesting that they have gone beyond their data in attempting to explain the discrepancy of employment between Catholic and Protestants:

Gudgin and Breen ask an interesting and important question - why are Catholics more than twice as likely to experience unemployment? …However, they misinterpret existing research findings and thereby use implausible assumptions which double count the factors which contribute to Catholic disadvantage. As a result, Gudgin and Breen provide the wrong answer to an important question. …Many readers of the paper will be tempted to ignore these issues and draw policy conclusions. For example, some may conclude that Catholics should migrate at over twice the rate of Protestants because their unemployment rate is twice as high, that Catholics should reduce their fertility or that the long term unemployed should be placed on job schemes, thereby 'solving' the problem… the Gudgin-Breen paper is rather naive from a policy perspective. (Ibid; P.76)

Recent government policy has gone one step beyond the sorts of job schemes mentioned above and introduced more or less compulsory 'welfare to work' programmes funded largely by taxing the public utilities such as gas, electricity and water that were privatised by the previous Conservative administration during the 1980s.

The argument that stresses the cultural differences between the two communities as an explanation of the conflict in Northern Ireland takes as one of its starting points the perception among Catholics that their Irishness had, in the past, somehow been devalued and supplanted by an over-representation of British ideas and values in official descriptions of Northern Ireland's history and culture. From an opposite viewpoint, Protestants have

32

largely seen Irishness as indistinguishable from republicanism and Catholicism. This perception can be best exemplified in the characteristically hostile attitude of Protestants towards any proposed extension of Irish language teaching into what they consider to be their schools; seeing such activity as deeply politicised and one which would lead to a diminution of the Protestant character of their schools which are, in fact, state owned and administered as well as officially non-denominational in ethos. By contrast, Irish until recently was taught in most Catholic post-primary schools and is strongly associated with the perception of their schools by Catholic teachers and parents as Irish in ethos and orientation.

In the past, the presence of Irish in most post-primary Catholic secondary schools, therefore, acted both as a defining characteristic of the schools' Irishness, and similarly as a powerful outward symbol of the distinctiveness of the Catholic tradition in the face of what, in the past, has been perceived as a hostile 'official' British/Protestant culture. The government's aim in introducing the cross-curricular themes is to counteract the process of politicisation of Protestant and Catholic cultures, and the animosity that it engenders, through a programme of curricular intervention. The politicisation of culture stems from the different definitions that people in Northern Ireland have of themselves as alternatively British or Irish and the general issue of the politics of identity.

The Politics of Identity

Irish historiography has been the most popular medium for the exploration of the origins and consequences of the different community identities and the politics that flow from them. These range from the very broad and comprehensive work of historians such as Lyons (1971) and Beckett (1966) and more recently Foster (1989) to highly specific analyses of particularly formative periods such as that given by Fiske (1985) for the period during the Second World War. Indeed, it would be difficult to discuss the two communities' approaches to their cultural heritage without some treatment of their respective 'histories', but the main focus here will be on the question of identity as a key element of those 'histories' which have shaped the experiences of the two groups, and the major ways in which their traditions have been defined, legitimated and transferred. The argument will concentrate chiefly on schools and the perceptions of employment opportunities as the most significant formative 'arenas' for the creation of both individual and community identities and their impact on the framing of education policy.

Firstly, as to the area of employment, the recently formed Fair Employment Commission has one over-riding statistic as its target for change; the fact that Catholics are on average twice as likely to be unemployed as their Protestant counterparts. This is something of an over-generalisation of the Commission's role in scrutinising patterns of recruitment where it very effectively reveals and attempts to counteract the way in which each community tends to 'look after its own' by employing either Protestant or Catholic co-religionists. Unlike its predecessor, the Fair Employment Agency, the Commission now has the power to compel employers, in their recruitment of employees, to be representative of the religious balance in the surrounding community. Discrimination has also been evident with regard to the different types of employment which have, in the past, been 'owned' by the two communities. Higher paid skilled manual workers in manufacturing industries, for instance, are recruited predominantly from the Protestant community; the lower paid, more seasonal and economically vulnerable building and construction workforce has been chiefly Catholic in nature. Identity, both individual and community, cannot but be influenced by these and other sorts of economic realities and the consequently different processes of socialisation experienced by Protestants and Catholics in their families, at work and in the wider community. The resulting attitudes are rarely articulated formally, but they deeply influence perceptions of employment and, more precisely, the opportunity structure available to young people. Concepts of power, control, authority and social equity form the basis of such attitudes and affect perceptions of self and of future employment prospects. More generally, they provide an important reference point for the way each community thinks about, uses, and consolidates its cultural heritage.

The central point here is that these variables produce significant differences between the two main religious groups in Northern Ireland and that they are likely to affect the characteristics of applicants for jobs and their performance at interviews, selection boards, and so on. Such attitudes will be manifest in the extent to which they see themselves as 'insiders' or 'outsiders' in the contest involving the major forms of employment and whether they feel themselves to be in control or being controlled in their life situation as well as their attitudes towards government intentions.

In summary, Catholic cultural heritage has been shaped by its relationship to power, control, and to questions of social and economic equity as well as to the status of Northern Ireland as a legitimate and just society. Much of this heritage has, in reality and of necessity, been a form of resistance to what has been seen as forms of Protestant economic and cultural domination. Cathcart (1984) gives a clear account of the way in which Protestant viewpoints became represented, through the BBC, as the ideal or official culture. This, he argues, resulted in the devaluation of forms of entertainment and the censoring of political discussion that was thought to reflect an Irish background. Britishness was the predominant lens through which broadcasting was examined and in a sense 'filtered'. Such an ideology was as damaging, in its way, to Protestants as it was dismissive of Catholic traditions since it gave Protestants a limited and impoverished view of themselves and their cultural heritage as Irish men and women by effectively defining the Irish sources of Protestant culture as strictly limited to the six counties of Northern Ireland. Cathcart gives an example of this process; he relates how in the late 1930s the introduction of music based on Irish folk tradition by the BBC proved controversial. The music was played by a group known as the 'Irish Rhythms' and was criticised as belonging to 'foreign culture'. The resulting programme outlived this early opposition and stayed on the air for 30 years and was regularly broadcast in Great Britain, Europe and throughout the world.

Education and Identity

Economic imperatives on their own cannot give a sufficient account or explanation of how a community develops a collective view of itself. The way in which such a view is sustained through schooling and leisure pursuits needs also to be examined if a full understanding is to be gained of the nature of the relationship between identity and heritage for both Protestants and Catholics and attempts through curriculum policy to improve attitudes towards each other's viewpoints. Many of those who try to explain Protestants' and Catholics' mistrust and suspicion of each other have devoted considerable attention to certain aspects of the school curriculum such as history, sport and, to some extent, music. In particular, the teaching of history has, in the past, been perceived to generate mutually prejudicial attitudes among very many Protestants and Catholics so that it became a vehicle for republican or loyalist indoctrination. Whatever the truth of this belief, it is arguable that recent changes in history teaching have made such an assertion more questionable; there is now a compulsory common curriculum for all schools. There are, however, other less publicly recognised differences in curriculum choices and preferences which are generated by the two identities in Northern Ireland. An example of this was highlighted in recent research evidence revealing important differences between Protestant and Catholics in a sample of 1,600 A level students in their preferences for science subjects despite government policy in encouraging the uptake of science and making it compulsory to age 16. Protestants at age 17 were studying these subjects in significantly larger numbers than Catholic boys, in addition to a marked gender disadvantage for Catholic girls.

Table 2.1 **Number of Maths/Science A levels taken by Catholic and Protestant Students**

No of A levels	Boys Protestant	Boys Catholic	Girls Protestant	Girls Catholic
0	97 28.8%	155 39.6%	170 29%	133 46.7%
1	62 18.4%	72 18.4%	174 29.6%	76 26.7%
2	68 20.2%	84 21.5%	113 19.3%	45 15.8%
3	84 24.9%	74 18.9%	111 18.9%	28 9.8%
4	26 7.%	6 1.5%	19 3.2%	3 1.1%
Totals	337 100%	391 100%	587 100%	285 100%
Mean no.	1.6	1.2	1.4	0.9
Taken	p<.001		p<.001	

Source: (Gallagher et al; 1995)

An initial reaction to this finding might be that the culture of Catholic post-primary schools is more humanities based than that of similar Protestant schools. One Catholic headmaster, on receiving the results, expressed his confidence in Catholic education for giving pupils a balanced curriculum. Ostensibly, such a viewpoint reflects traditional thinking about the need for an even-handed intellectual approach with regard to arts and science subjects.

In this case, it has the unintended effect of deflecting attention from the problem of imbalance that exists between the two communities in terms of their respective intellectual 'property' and the consequences for Catholic students' future employment opportunities. Other similar findings indicate that the ideal of 'balance' in the curriculum of Catholic schools unintentionally narrows the employment choices of their pupils with respect to those careers which require a basis of scientific training and knowledge (Osborne et al; 1987). With regard to more general patterns of economic power and cultural primacy, differences between Protestants and Catholics in their uptake of science have been reflected in the differential allocation of jobs and the representation of the two communities' 'histories'.

With respect to the exercise of power, it is closely, though not solely, bound up with the control of the opportunities structure where Northern Ireland Protestants, have achieved, for historical reasons, a degree of monopoly over the better paid and higher status occupations. Such patterns and practices of discrimination are now illegal with respect to employers' recruitment policies, but their past effects still substantially exist in the extent to which Catholics' and Protestants' choices are influenced by the over or under-representation of their co-religionists at a particular factory or institution. This is often referred to as the 'chill factor'. These choices are also sustained through the traditional cultural and educational heritage of each community as they are expressed in their schools' academic ambience and their pupils' intellectual preferences. Engineering and technological jobs are a case in point where, in the past, there have been disproportionately fewer Catholic workers which may, therefore, have resulted in a lack of emphasis on science and technology in Catholic schools, since the opportunity structure, for wider political reasons, was weighted against Catholic employment in these types of jobs. In addition, Catholic schools, because of their voluntary status had to raise 15% of their capital costs until 1992 (in the past there was a larger percentage to be raised). Science laboratories are necessarily expensive to build and the Catholic authorities have been faced with the task of raising substantial amounts of money to build such facilities from a population that was already economically disadvantaged. Whilst there is no direct evidence available, it would seem reasonable, on this historical basis, to expect some degree of under-provision of science laboratories in the Catholic school system.

In summary, the arguments in this section have set out to analyse the question of cultural identity within the wider contexts of employment, politics and schooling. They are based on the view that, if cross curricular themes such as cultural heritage and education for mutual understanding are to effect

37

any changes in the communities' perceptions, understanding and treatment of each other, it must be based on a deeper analysis of their respective Protestant and Catholic identities. It is important to go beyond definitions of cultural identity and heritage which rely solely on historical and educational premises. The view taken here is that each community has developed a particular pattern of meaning systems based on their different cultural, educational and economic experiences. These involve values, inclinations and attitudes towards crucial areas such as power, social and economic equity and ultimately the legitimisation of the state's political, legal, moral and economic purposes.

Government policy in introducing and continuing to support,cultural heritage and education for mutual understanding programmes in schools is evidence in itself that it intends to create a heterodoxy in the definitions of culture and, particularly, in the treatment by schools of the different and often antipathetic perceptions which Catholics and Protestants have of each other's traditions. The policy represents a timely recognition of the need for an initiative in the whole area of defining cultures on the basis of what the two groups share in their backgrounds. This is a radical shift from former culturally arbitrary approaches to an alternative cultural pattern which challenges what were represented in the past as 'official' or 'ideal' definitions of culture and which were in reality predominately Unionist in orientation. The curricular programmes attempt to promote the two heritages as being of equal value and highlight what they share and the large area of overlap between the two traditions. In doing so, it will at least diminish the degree of past 'symbolic violence' towards Catholic cultural heritage by promoting it through the schools as an integral part of the state's culture and legitimate meaning systems (Bourdieu; 1988). The converse is equally true with regard to Catholic pupils' appreciation of Protestant traditions as the programmes are introduced to their schools and may eventually go some way towards a redefinition of Protestant and Catholic cultures where Unionism and Nationalism can co-exist.

In the past, the power structure in Ulster has worked in such a way as to marginalise those who asserted their right to an alternative identity. In some instances this assertion has been used to explain the disadvantages under which Catholics labour in relation to equality of employment opportunities. It has been argued that the Catholic authorities' insistence on maintaining a separate school system has contributed to Catholic disabilities. A former Minister of Home Affairs in the Stormont Government before it was prorogued in 1972, went so far as to suggest that the under-representation of Catholics on the judiciary was the result of the lower competence of Catholic lawyers (Kennedy; 1971).

Catholics, particularly from manual working backgrounds, did not fully apprehend how the system worked beyond having the feeling that their religion somehow labelled them as being less employable than their Protestant counterparts. This point, however, needs to be set in the context of the overall economic disadvantage of Northern Ireland as a region; a situation which affected both Protestants and Catholics, but the net result was an unequal experience of disadvantage and unemployment in the case of the Catholic community. Poverty was a way of life for both working class communities but the difference for Catholics was that the labelling referred to the religious and cultural qualities of individuals and their community: that they had somehow brought this on themselves because of their adherence to Nationalist forms of culture and politics in addition to the poverty that also affected their Protestant counterparts. Such a process deflected attention away from the province's failure both as an economic unit and in its toleration of widespread patterns of discrimination. Protestants, by contrast, have as a community experienced a continuity between their cultural processes and heritage, on the one hand, and the meanings and cultural symbols of dominance as they were expressed through their schools, through politics in the unbroken sequence of Unionist governments since 1921 and also in the media which in the past were predominantly British in orientation. Notable exceptions were newspapers such as the Irish News which gave voice to Nationalist politics, culture and sport.

Curricular Intervention: Future Projections

The likely outcomes of the policy of promoting cultural and political understanding through schooling will, from the outset, be heavily influenced by the analysis of conflict in Northern Ireland, on which the policy's recommendations for action in schools is based. The argument so far has been that only a partial analysis of the sources of prejudice and mistrust has been offered by official bodies such as the original cultural heritage and education for mutual understanding working groups which set out the curricular guidelines. In its report, the original group describe cultural heritage, for example, broadly as 'humble domestic and farm utensils as well as great literature, art and music'. There is no adequate theory of conflict in such an approach other than a belief that it is a purely cultural phenomenon with its roots in Protestants' and Catholics' ignorance of their respective traditions as expressed in different choices of literature, music (to some extent) and, in the case of Catholics, participation in Gaelic sports.

The central argument here is that there is another deeper reality which needs to be analysed and confronted if government policy is to make successful inroads into present and future levels of misunderstanding and community tension. This other reality concerns the causes of and attitudes towards social and economic inequity as it affects people's future job opportunities as well as the overall economic and cultural standing of their respective communities. Appreciation of each other's traditions and aspirations will only be fully realised when, in addition to the policy's emphasis on ameliorating cultural prejudices and mutual misunderstanding, other more deeply rooted and manifest forms of inequity such as economic and social discrimination are also fully explored.

The strength of the current policy lies in its potential to enable Protestants and Catholics to confront some of the sources of their respective misunderstandings and prejudices about each other. Central to this process will be some sort of appreciation and comprehension of what Irishness means to members of both communities. For many Protestants this issue is not apparent since they would not consider themselves to be Irish, preferring to be known solely as British, whilst simultaneously distinguishing themselves from the other national identities of Great Britain. In Northern Ireland, no enduring consensus concerning Irishness has emerged which could provide any real basis for both Protestants and Catholics beginning to feel identified as primarily Northern Irish, or Ulster as a cultural and political identity. The two educational intervention programmes of cultural heritage and education for mutual understanding are a welcome attempt to build a basis for each community to understand the other's viewpoints and aspirations.

Another of the policy's strengths lies in the way the curricular programmes it has generated deal with the source of this fracture of identity by asking both groups to stop looking only to sources outside the province for characteristics of their communities; what Whyte called the 'exogenous' explanation. While there are individual exceptions, Protestants have looked chiefly to British sources whilst Catholics, sceptical of the moral and political validity of Northern Ireland, have traditionally given primacy to Irish sources in the creation of a common Catholic heritage. This is best exemplified by the different and politically mutually exclusive events which Protestants and Catholics commemorate and in the case of parades by the Orange Order are the source of so much conflict during the annual 'marching season'. These chiefly entail triumphalist celebrations dating back to the Williamite wars of the 17th century. Such a background provides a bleak landscape for the development of a common cultural heritage. Since the onset of the present Troubles, the area for compromise between the two groups has grown progressively more narrow under the impact of sectarian murders and larger atrocities such as 'Bloody Sunday' in 1972 or the more recent Enniskillen bombing and the tensions generated during the 'marching season', where international attention and media are focused on places such as Dumcree, the Apprectice Boys commemoration of the relief of Londonderry and the other marching flashpoints in the province. The absence of consensus with regard to the legitimacy of the annual Orange Order parades is a violent outward demonstration of a deeper community based disagreement about identity. The parades strengthen the vacuum of agreed cultural and political structures of Northern Ireland. It leaves only a limited foundation on which social solidarity can be built. The continuing policy of cross curricular themes can only improve this situation through its emphasis on pupils studying those aspects of their traditions which they share.

The educational themes policy has a formidable task before it. Perhaps its initial handicap lay in the incomplete analysis of the cultural traditions on which the programme is premised. The present argument has been that political and economic discrimination together with 'symbolic violence' with regard to a lack of tolerance of different cultures, have contributed towards two cultural traditions which have few significant points of contact. The policy requires a harder edge with regard to the more material sources of mistrust and prejudice through, for example, looking more closely at the work of the Commission for Racial Equality in Great Britain and similar agencies in America and the European Community. The framers of the programme have already gone some way to providing this international perspective by including, in its objectives, a consideration of the work of the United Nations, Greenpeace and of underprivileged minorities in the United States of America (Hispanics) and Germany (Turks). Additionally, teachers are asked to compare the Northern Ireland conflict with other societies with similar problems such as Cyprus and the Basque region.

Conclusion: Segregation and Identity

The fact that there are effectively two quite separate school systems in terms of enrolments, one predominantly Protestant and one almost wholly Catholic, in Northern Ireland is a further limiting factor in the achievement of the government policy. Separateness on the part of the Catholic authorities is justified on the grounds of freedom of religious conscience. Attacks on their insistence in maintaining their own schools as distinctively Catholic in character and ethos are perceived by many as a threat to the right to pursue the Catholic religion itself. The fact of separation, however, provides a suitable context in which, through mono-cultural and religious friendships, the hidden curriculum of prejudice and mistrust can frustrate Catholic and also Protestant teachers' ostensible aims of religious and cultural tolerance. Its most striking form lies in the creation of a group identity among Protestant and Catholic pupils which accentuates the extremes of the opposite community. This relates to perceptions of their political views, discrimination practices in employment and, not least, their propensity for physical attack through sectarian violence. Such views emerge most strikingly during critical periods where one community feels itself to be particularly threatened. The Ulster Workers' strike of 1974, the republican prisoners' hunger strike of 1982, and the signing of The Anglo-Irish Agreement of 1985, the Downing Street Declaration of 1993 as well as the recurring violence during the summer parades season, are examples of such occasions.

One of the ways in which the cross-curricular programmes attempt to dismantle community based attitudes and prejudices towards the 'other side' is by setting them in an international context. This trans-national theme is pursued throughout the programmes' guidelines; at age 16, for instance, pupils when studying history, should also know about 20th century trans-national organisations such as the United Nations Organisation, the World health Organisation, and Greenpeace as part of both their history and Cultural heritage syllabuses. In a similar way, teachers are asked to examine Irish migration in the context of the Dutch in South Africa, penal colonies in Australia and Hispanics in the United States of America. More recently, the commemoration of the Irish Famine which began in 1845 was set against the context of similar catastrophes of the twentieth century such famines in Ethopia and Somalia. Displays in museums and other educational initiatives set historical figures of starving Irish men and women alongside similar representations of Ethopians and Somalis who have recently experienced similar catastrophes.

To the extent that the policy achieves its aim of promoting greater understanding among Protestants and Catholics, it is to be welcomed as an antidote to both curricular and street based history. The method involves an enlargement of the frame for understanding to include European and international dimensions of Protestant and Catholic cultural heritages. Such a process, however, is also one of the programme's weaknesses in so far as it lacks a real critical edge in its avoidance or neglect of deeper sources of identity and community tension. These, it has been argued, are to be found in the different experiences of Protestants and Catholics with regard to fundamental life experiences such as employment, their different attitudes towards power and social equity, and, lastly, their perceptions of the legitimacy and justness of the society itself.

3 Structure, Power and Policy

The Northern Ireland School System

Throughout the 19th century and for the first twenty years of the present one, England, Scotland, Wales and the whole of Ireland existed as the United Kingdom. The shared history of the two islands meant that until 1870 they developed, in certain areas, similar policies with regard to the administration and management of their schools. In Ireland however, there was no equivalent to the Education Acts of 1870 and 1902 which laid the basis for a largely state system in England and Wales. As discussed in chapter one Irish education, until 1921, was administered mainly by Church authorities through their control of the National Schools. They have remained influential in the management of schools to the present day. In chapter one it was also argued that, as a result of retaining the union with Westminster in 1921, the Northern Ireland government developed a 'step-by-step' policy with respect to educational changes made by central government in England and Wales. The 1944 Act in Great Britain, for example, was mirrored by similar legislation in Northern Ireland and again in 1988, the Education Reform Act for England and Wales was followed in 1989 by the broadly similar Education (N.I.) Reform Order. The province's education system does, however, have a number of distinguishing features which make it markedly different from the Scottish, English and Welsh systems. The most important aspects are:

- a dual system of schooling consisting of 'controlled' schools owned and run by public authorities and attended predominantly by Protestants and a large voluntary sector owned and governed jointly by the Catholic Church and public representitives. Since 1992 these have been wholly funded by the state. In addition, there are 54 voluntary grammar schools;

- for an area of its size and population, Northern Ireland is served by a greater diversity of school authorities than any comparable region within the United Kingdom. As well as the Department of Education for Northern Ireland (DENI), there are five Education and Library Boards (ELBs), the Commission for Catholic Maintained Schools (CCMS), the

Northern Ireland Council for Integrated Education (NICIE) and the non-statutory Governing Bodies Association for Northern Ireland (GBA) which represents, but has no responsibility for the individual interests of 54 voluntary grammar schools which deal individually and directly with DENI;

- transfer from primary to secondary education for the majority of pupils is based on a selection test at 11. There are two types of schools at secondary level, grammar (selective) and secondary (non-selective);

- an absence of any significant number of independent sector schools; and

- the members of the Education and Library Boards are appointed by the Secretary of State, they are nominated by DENI, the churches and District Councils. On any ELB only a minority (40%) of members are drawn from elected representatives from the District Councils.

In chapter one it was argued that this system emerged from historical, cultural and religious factors present in the 19th century and the earlier part of the present one. Its most outwardly visible features are a division between schools on the basis of religious affiliation and, on the basis of a selection test (the 11+), with respect to the type of school (grammar or secondary) after the age of eleven. The Churches, both Catholic and Protestant, exercise considerable influence on schooling in Northern Ireland. The Catholic Church does so through its ownership of the voluntary maintained primary and secondary schools and more than half the voluntary grammar schools. The influence of the Protestant Church is more diffuse, being based on the rights of representation on boards of governors of controlled schools as discussed in chapter one. These were granted after 1930 when they transferred their schools to the local education authorities. They are also a significant presence in the management of voluntary grammar schools. Government policy-making in education is therefore conducted against a background of Church interests whose authority is based largely on their representativeness of wider Protestant and Catholic political power. The denominational basis of schooling is perceived and supported by the two communities as a powerful means of preserving their respective cultural and religious traditions.

One conclusion that can be drawn from the structure above is that, in size and population, Northern Ireland retains a significantly more elaborate administrative system than similar Local Education Authorities in Great

Britain. In one sense, it is a reflection of the history of Northern Ireland and the community divisions that have arisen. But in another, such a system will inevitably incur higher running costs, funds that could be used more effectively in an area with high levels of social and educational disadvantage. The position is, however, somewhat anomalous given the higher overall amount allocated to education as one aspect of Northern Ireland's public expenditure which, in 1994-95, stood at around 10% compared to the average of 5% of GDP for the rest of the United kingdom. This is partly explained by the larger numbers of children attending schools and, at the upper end of the age range, higher post 16 participation, especially university education. Despite the greater proportion of public finances spent on education as a whole, an imbalance occurs in the lower level of funds allocated per capita to nursery and primary schools: in Northern Ireland this was £1,285 compared to £1,472 in England. The respective figures for secondary pupils are £2,039 and £2,145 (DENI; 1994, P.24).

In its major policy document 'Learning for Life' (1994) from which these figures are derived, there is no justification for this allocation of funds and the differentials that they produce. It would seem reasonable to argue that the top-heavy administrative structure draws off funds to pay for Board and Department officials, advisers, teachers and other support staff needed to run what, in effect, are two parallel, but religiously segregated systems. These are funds that might otherwise be spent directly on pupils and their schools. One consequence of denominational separation is the proliferation of small schools: a secondary school in the province with under 450 pupils would be officially considered small whereas the comparable figure in Great Britain is 600.

The practical outcome and funding implications of segregation are evident typically in the mid-Ulster town of Dungannon with a population of 45,000 which until 1995 was served by three primary schools, seven post-primary schools and one College of Further Education. This group breaks down as: separate single-sex Catholic grammar, secondary and primary schools (six schools), one voluntary grammar, one secondary school and one primary school all predominantly Protestant. The total enrolment is 5,292 giving a crude average of 480 per school, just above what would be considered a small school (Source; 1991 Census). There is also a newly formed integrated primary school just outside the town boundary drawing pupils from Dungannon and surrounding district which is also funded by the DENI. The aggregated salary, administrative, capital and running costs of the 12 separate institutions in and around Dungannon and other similar locations in 1995 explain in large measure

47

the apparent anomaly of a bigger global sum spent on education than elsewhere in Great Britain, whilst a smaller amount actually reaches the pupil in the classroom. The deficits of spending on pupils in percentages are 14.5% less per pupil in primary schools than England and Wales and 2.5% at secondary level (Northern Ireland Economic Council 1995). Since 1995, the two Catholic primary schools have amalgamated and the Catholic secondary schools are in the process of forming one school.

Small school size creates other hidden costs with respect to capital costs where in Northern Ireland these take up 5.3% of public expenditure compared with 3.5%, 3.9% and 3.4% for similar sizes authorities in England, Wales and Scotland respectively (CSO; 1994. P.62). The Northern Ireland Economic Council (1995) has argued that reducing the number of small schools in Northern Ireland in line with the pattern in Scotland which has probably a more dispersed population, would represent a saving of approximately £20m (P.130). In policy terms the Department has set out to rationalise the provision of small primary schools on educational grounds as well as their increased costs compared with larger units. The argument is based on the view that their small size militates against the full coverage of the Northern Ireland Curriculum, and a more general assumption that they were somehow failing in their ability to offer the full range of social, cultural and recreational relationships and activities available in a larger school. The implied but rarely articulated ideal type seems often to conform to a suburban mid-sized primary school, and takes little account of the importance of the different social and cultural functions of a small rural school as a focus for the local population's perception of itself, in a sense, its worth or standing as a viable community. This is doubly so in the context of the mostly Protestant communities living in predominantly Catholic areas near the border with the Republic. In the predominantly Catholic Western and Southern Boards 58% and 68%, of Protestant pupils respectively are in schools with an enrolment of less than 100. The comparable percentages for Catholic pupils are 40 and 43, Gallagher (1993b).

The Rural Development Council for Northern Ireland has argued that the spread of population is such that it would be difficult to close large numbers of small primary schools and that there are now very few schools of under 50 pupils, leading to the view that only relatively small amounts could be saved from further large scale closures (Ibid). The Council in its review of small schools also suggests that the curricular 'deficit' argument is unsound, that the evidence in this respect shows the schools have a good record. In support of this view the Council Report 'Small Primary Schools' published in

1993, quotes evidence from research conducted in Northern Ireland and Great Britain arguing that small schools place no implicit curricular restrictions on their pupils because of their size and offered additional benefits, according to Caul and Harbison (1989), with better opportunities for learning social and personal skills. This finding was supported by Galton (1990) who revealed that subject spread in small primary schools in Great Britain was comparable to provision in larger schools. Assumptions about lack of provision, he argued, for subjects such as science or humanities were unfounded.

One recent factor is the central involvement of the teaching principal in ensuring the quality of teaching the new curriculum and the extent of its coverage in contrast, it is suggested, to the more distanced 'walking' or non-teaching headteacher in the larger schools and the fact that such longer serving principals often have little or no direct experience of teaching the new syllabuses and programmes introduced since 1989. In addition, the assumed limitations of resources in small primary school will be obviated by the introduction of the National Grid for Learning when every school will be connected to the World Wide Web. Despite the best efforts of the Council to argue that there is little to be gained financially in wholesale closures of small schools, they remain more expensive in terms of per-capita costs. These have been calculated as:

Table 3.1   Average per Pupil Allocation by Size of School in Northern Ireland, 1993-94

	50 and under	51-100	101-200	200 plus
Primary Costs £ per pupil	1,850	1,457	1,332	1,237
	400 and under	400-800	800-1000	1000 plus
Secondary Costs £ per pupil	2,509	2,127	2,028	2,077

Source: Northern Ireland Economic Council (1995)

The Northern Ireland Economic Council suggests that savings of £20m could be made if the pattern of school enrolment above was brought into line with Scotland where there is a similarly dispersed population. This argument makes no provision for the fact that, whilst denominational schooling is a more prominent feature of Scotland's system than in England and Wales, it dominates the structure of schooling in Northern Ireland to a much greater extent. The result in Northern Ireland is two parallel systems of Catholic and Protestant schools both of which need to be funded from public expenditure.

The direct impact of having to spread resources to meet the demands of the greater number of small and average sized schools in a segregated system impose an opportunity cost on other parts of the system; there will be less money for other types of school. This is also evident in the amount of money spent on nursery education where Northern Ireland trails behind the rest of the UK despite its acknowledged long-term educational and social benefits and the high levels of regional disadvantage in these areas.

Table 3.2   Three and Four Year Olds in Public Sector Schools, 1992

	Pupils in nursery schools and nursery classes and participation rate		Pupils in infant classes in primary schools and participation rate	
	Age 3 Thous (%)	Age 4 Thous (%)	Age 3 Thous (%)	Age 4 Thous (%)
England	247 (37.7)	55 (8.7)	1 (0.2)	299 (47.3)
Wales	16 (41.6)	10 (25.3)	1 (3.7)	24 (62.1)
Scotland	12 (18.6)	32 (49.2)	0 (0)	9 (14.5)
N.Ireland	**4 (15.0)**	**4 (14.8)**	**0 (0)**	**17 (63.1)**

Source: National Commission on Education (1993; P. 123) *(Author's emphasis)*

These figures show that of the Northern Ireland children receiving education in this age range, most are in infant or Key Stage one classes. The figures confirm that, in the case of three year olds at nursery schools, Northern Ireland has the lowest participation rate, effectively depriving a larger number of children than elsewhere in the country of the advantages of early childhood education. Additionally, a large percentage of four-year-olds appear to be introduced to formal education at what many argue is too early a stage and where the teaching is not appropriate to their needs. This looks short-sighted in the face of the evidence of the long-term benefits of nursery education above and beyond the immediate learning advantages of preparing children for the more academically formal atmosphere of the primary school. Research in the United States of America suggests that attendance at nursery school has greatest benefit when the learning atmosphere is concentrated on social and communicational skills rather than concentrating on learning to read and write. In economic terms, the estimate was that every dollar spent on nursery type education led to a later social 'profit' of seven dollars in savings on police, prison, and probation service costs. Pre-school pupils, in other words, made better, more law abiding citizens and generated more tax revenue as their employment opportunities were also enhanced, (Commission for Social Justice; 1994)

Other research conducted in the Republic of Ireland suggests that pupils aged 16 and over who had attended a nursery school were twice as likely to go on to further education or training than pupils with no pre-school experience. This trend, surprisingly, was not affected by their academic attainment (Kellaghan and Greaney; 1993). Given Northern Ireland's high levels of social disadvantage and unemployment, pre-school education would seem to be an area where government investment could render long-term benefits affecting not only the social and economic life of the province but also improvements in the quality of individuals' lives. The Northern Ireland Economic Council (1995) has calculated that, on the basis of estimated expenditure of £860m needed to bring the United Kingdom's nursery education up to European levels of provision, the equivalent figure for Northern Ireland would be £30m. Current spending on pre-school education is £8.8m representing 1.1% of funds allocated to the Boards whilst home-school transport costs £33.4 m which has increased latterly as a consequence of open enrolment, (Source; NIEC; 1997). The Department has recognised the imbalance and has decided to reduce these costs with no guarantee that savings will go to fund more nursery schools. Recent moves by central government to give every four-year-old a pre-school place has forced the DENI's hand on this matter in an announcement by the minister for education of a 20% increase in the number of nursery places (DENI; 1998).

In this context, the minister responsible for education has publicly floated the view that the government is considering removing funding of £1.5m for the fee-paying, semi-private preparatory departments attached to the Protestant grammar schools after local criticism that it amounted to a subsidy for Protestant middle class children being paid from public funds. Especially so when a local newspaper carried an article calculating how many nursery places could be provided by the amount going to the schools. Preparatory school supporters argue that the state system would have an extra burden in having to fund places for children transferring from the preparatory schools in the event of their closure. In the past, these schools or departments were perceived by parents as a means of easing their children's passage into the highly prized senior grammar school, especially if their child performed poorly at the 11+ test. This assumption was made on the grounds that the headteacher of the upper school would make a special case for 'one of its own'. Competition for grammar school places in recent years as a result of open enrolment is such that this 'backdoor' into what are highly prized schools has largely gone, although there is the grey area where family connections to a school could be weighed in a preparatory pupil's favour. In addition, the grammar schools, like the primaries and secondaries, are acutely aware of the importance of the annual league tables showing their academic results. The selective schools are therefore anxious to monitor the quality of the intake at transfer from their primary schools leading, at present, to an informal hierarchy of schools according to the 11+ grades of their intakes. This is based on parents' local information networks as they estimate the likely grade requirements of their children's intended schools and has real consequences for schools as their reputation for accepting either high or low grades gains currency among transferring parents and the wider community.

Policy Making and Direct Rule

Policy-making in Northern Ireland is widely perceived as being more centralised than in other parts of the United Kingdom such as Scotland and Wales. As in those two countries ultimate power resides with the Secretary of State advised by the minister responsible for education. There are, however, a number of features peculiar to Northern Ireland. One of these is the present system of direct rule from Westminster since the suspension of the Stormont Parliament in 1972. As a result, no local MPs act as ministers within any of the departments of government in Northern Ireland in contrast with arrangements in Scotland and Wales where Scottish and Welsh MPs serve in the their respective Offices. In addition, local politicians are elected to Local Education Authorities and have responsibility for spending locally raised taxes on schooling. In consequence, all government departments in Northern Ireland are run by ministers whose political base is on the British mainland. This creates an impression of rule from a more distant centre which is strengthened by the fact that legislation dealing specifically with Northern Ireland is dealt with by Orders in Council on the authority of the Privy Council rather than by full debate on the floor of the House of Commons, the normal procedure for Parliamentary Bills. Such Orders cannot be amended and this restriction is seen by some to add to the sense of remoteness. Government sensitivity to this perception was recently realised in the creation of the Northern Ireland Committee as part of the House of Commons' committee reporting system. Whilst it cannot debate the framing of legislation, the committee can, however, question politicians and officials on the implementation of Orders in Council and in this way improve the level of accountability of Northern Ireland Office politicians, local civil servants and other officials.

As a measure of being governed 'from afar', many people describe recent educational reform as 'an English answer to an English problem' and note that the Scots, who have avoided the straitjacket of a statutory curriculum, although now much amended in the rest of Great Britain, have been able to arrange their educational reforms in a different way. Of 248 school principals who responded to a questionnaire item that 'Direct Rule has increased the tendency for English formulas to be transplanted to Northern Ireland without regard for local peculiarities', 86% agreed and only 0.8% disagreed. An even larger group (96%) agreed with the proposition that 'Educational policy in Northern Ireland is largely determined by what happens in England and Wales' (Leckey; 1993).

An additional factor is the different structure of local government in Northern Ireland and the restricted scope of its responsibilities. Since 1972 there has been no equivalent to the relationship which existed, at its best, as a partnership in Great Britain until recent years between local authorities and schools. The province's education service is administered by five Education and Library Boards of whose members only a minority are drawn from local government councillors: they are nominated by the Secretary of State rather than elected directly to the Boards' education committees. This is the only structural provision made for representation of local political interests. District councillors, however, do wield considerably more influence than their minority position might suggest. This is partly explained by their status as elected representatives, but just as importantly, their knowledge of local circumstances which, in the context of direct rule, is largely unavailable to Northern Ireland Office ministers. They also represent the one legitimating democratic element in an otherwise representative but non-democratic public body. Another important factor is that since all Board finances come directly from central government the councillors do not have to be concerned about how their espousal of particular policies are likely to affect local rates.

Features such as these go some way to explaining the perception of policy-making as somewhat remote and centralist. While the interview research to be set out later in the book indicates dissatisfaction with present arrangements, it must be borne in mind that the causes of discontent arise from factors which have as much to do with Northern Ireland's general political situation as those which relate directly to decision-making in education. Two of the Boards have, for example, developed a policy to protect the funding of small Protestant schools in border areas which are expensive in terms of unit costs per pupil, a policy that has educational, cultural and political contexts. The extent of its support by local Catholic and Protestant politicians and other representatives can be gauged by the fact that the areas covered by the Boards are pre-dominantly Nationalist yet they receive broad cross-cultural co-operation for their approach.

In recent times centralist tendencies in educational policy have not been confined to Northern Ireland and there are also particular circumstances which offset or mitigate such policies. One of these is the relatively small size of the province in relation to both geographical area and population. It is approximately as large as some of the bigger local government areas in England and its population consists of approximately a million and a half people. This makes for a good deal of informal contact between various interest groups in education with a tradition of reasonably easy access to government ministers and civil servants. The value of this practice is generally recognised by teachers and officials alike and can result in the sort of accommodation over small border area Protestant schools set out above. There is also agreement that direct rule has operated to the general advantage of Northern Ireland in a period of financial stringency.

The Department of Education

Direct rule has placed the Department of Education for Northern Ireland (DENI) in a unique position vis-a-vis its equivalent in the Welsh and Scottish Offices in the extent to which it acts as a regional authority unaccountable to local democratic bodies, whilst responsible for aspects of education including the payment of teachers' salaries, the Education and Library Boards' funds, the curriculum, and the framing of educational policy. Against this background a culture of officialdom has been not so much created as strengthened, the Department both proposes and disposes in a more direct way than elsewhere in Great Britain. At the same time, there have been some benefits from the imposition of direct rule with respect to the introduction of the cross-curricular programmes discussed earlier which are designed to decrease community mistrust and dispel sectarian myths about 'the other side'. It is arguable that there would have been considerable disagreement and debate over their content relating to the Churches' and local politicians' interests in protecting their constituencies' cultures and identities. The almost inevitable consequence would have been considerable delay and dilution of what are innovative attempts to promote social consensus through education. Another case is the creation of a system of integrated schools for which the Department now has a statutory duty to promote and fund.

In developing these schools the Department is returning to the policy of the National Schools of the 19th century: in effect, making a third way in an otherwise tightly segregated system of denominational schooling. DENI is also demonstrating its independence in the face of considerable pressure from the Protestant Churches to establish a Transferors' Representative Council as means of matching the Catholic Church's influence through its majority on the Council for Catholic Maintained Schools (CCMS). They have applied the same argument with regard to the formal representation of the integrated sector's interests by the Northern Ireland Council for Integrated Education (NICIE). The Protestant Churches see this also as a means of furthering Protestant interests in the state schools. Since 1989 CCMS has been the employing authority for all teachers in the Catholic maintained sector and also advises on a wide range of matters including recruitment, appointment of senior staff and in strategic planning, including advice on replies to inspection. Whilst it does not constitute a sixth Board, nevertheless, in carrying out the tasks above, it has taken on a number of their key functions. The Protestant Churches argue that in comparison to the other sectors they are now seriously disadvantaged in their 'stewardship' of the state schools, a responsibility assumed, they argue, when transferring their schools to the state in 1925 and 1930.

The Department is currently resisting pressure from the Protestant Churches for a Transferors' Council and McKeown and Byrne (1998) quotes an official reflecting the Department's view:

> The Transferors raised the idea that controlled schools were church-related schools, but no, they are state schools open to atheists, Jews, Catholics and anybody who wants to attend them; and the teachers are as entitled as anybody else to be anything, or nothing in terms of religious affiliation. There is no likelihood that the basic structures will change, that we will hand the controlled schools back to the Protestant Churches to run. (P.21)

In summary, it is clear that, in terms of the formulation and implementation of educational policies, Northern Ireland is similar to other parts of the United Kingdom. It is, however, perceived by many people in the province as too heavily centralised and too strongly influenced by what happens in England and Wales. The underlying 'step-by-step' ideology of this approach in one sense goes as far back as partition in 1921 and the new Unionist government's determination to align the province's politics and social and educational systems closely to those in Great Britain. Its other more practical purpose, still relevant today, was to ensure equal treatment of people in Northern Ireland compared to their British counterparts and that their educational qualifications had currency in Great Britain when applying there for jobs or higher education places.

The argument here is that the pre-eminent role of DENI in funding schools, the local boards, paying teachers and its responsibility for policy has been significantly strengthened by the advent of direct rule since 1972, but without the checks and balances of local democratically based politics. At the same time, there is evidence of a degree of independence in its relations with the Churches, especially the Protestant denominations in curtailing any further increase in the their influence over the state schools.

The centrality of the Department's role in administering and funding all levels of education whilst remaining outside the direct scrutiny of locally elected councillors, found elsewhere in Great Britain, is usually interpreted benignly. The relationship, it is argued, is marked by the rarity of serious disputes between the local boards, CCMS and the Department and other educational interests, largely attributable, it is claimed, to the high levels of access to government officials available to schools, appointed local councillors and members of other local educational agencies in a small area similar in size to a large local authority in England. Local board and CCMS members and the Department's officials, it is often argued (Leckey; 1993), share similar professional values as a basis for administering the system. McKeown (1993) quotes an interview with a Board official in this respect:

> The distinction between the Education and Library Boards and the Department is sometimes more illusory then real. The DfEE and DES local authorities are very different…here you tend to get a lot of strong consensus at the professional level before any issues ever arise. And the Department mostly…tries to take the…Boards with them. So generally speaking, you do not get these major disputes. (P.94)

The Education and Library Boards

The existence of five Education and Library Boards for a population of one and a half million has led to an argument that, in comparison to Great Britain, the province's education system is over-administered and, in the context of closer scrutiny by governments of public expenditure, does not represent 'value for money'. There is a general perception of the Boards as overly bureaucratic structures with little impact on policy-making irrespective of the constraints of direct rule. More positively, however, they have built up considerable administrative expertise and they are responsive to local needs through a combination of local politicians and clergy, both Catholic and Protestant. They provide a forum representative of groups and interests which would not otherwise have come together given existing community divisions. One of the politicians interviewed for the research for this book conceded that while there might be a degree of over-administration this phenomenon was not uncommon in other countries in Europe where there were ethnic or religious divisions. He cited Holland and Switzerland as examples and suggested that in such circumstances the ensuing financial cost might be offset by gains in social stability.

There is a more general view among educationists in the region and in the Department that a 'second tier' in the structure of education administration is needed in Northern Ireland. The alternative of a direct relationship between each school and the DENI is unrealistic. Such an arrangement seems to work well enough for the 54 voluntary grammar schools in the province but, apart from logistical implications for DENI, it would further reinforce the centralist features of the system. It would also, for example, be to the disadvantage of the many small primary schools (chiefly in rural areas) and lead to greater unevenness in the quality of school management and resource provision. Board members also provide some degree of balance against central executive power where so many responsibilities have come into its remit since the introduction of direct rule in 1972.

It is also arguable that the Boards have not acted in any significantly innovative way. The point of their creation in 1973 coincided with the introduction of direct rule and a seemingly inexorable shift of power to the centre in the management and funding of the school system. Despite this tendency there has been some diversification in so far as individual Boards have built up strengths in specific areas of school activity such as information technology and music. They also exercise discretion in a range of administrative decisions. An example is the application of formula funding under Local Management of Schools (LMS). DENI Circular 1990/10 'permits and expects' Boards to take account of factors such as the protection of small schools, special needs and social deprivation in applying the formula and they do this on an individual basis. Important as decisions like these are, they are matters of fine-tuning rather than initiative. One of the chief factors in this is the Boards' total dependence on government for tightly prescribed funds through the process of 'ring-fencing' of budgets and accountability for their use. The absence of any additional or more flexible source such as might be provided by local rates is a substantial constraint on possible innovation. In addition, the funding procedures which are conducted on a mainly annual basis are regarded as inhibiting long-term planning. One of the Board's Chief Executive Officers summed-up their position:

> There is actually a negation of the whole concept of public and local authority which is set-up in principle to determine local needs and to meet those needs in the best and most efficient way…Boards have a fair amount of independence from DENI provided; they do not run into overspends; they do not work against government policy; they interpret their spend patterns as the Board thinks fit. (Leckey; 1993. P.19)

The viewpoint expressed here shows the constraints placed upon Boards by the Department's role as their 'banker'. The degree of independence being determined by adherence to public policy seems legitimate with respect to the normal local and national democratic underpinning of government departments. In the case of the DENI, however, half of the equation is missing with local agencies and schools having recourse only to Westminster MPs who exercise power in education, but whose constituencies are outside the province and who are not directly accountable to the electorate of Northern Ireland in the same way as local politicians would be. A recent notable and successful exercise of independence occurred when the DENI decided to reduce the number of Education and Library Boards from five to three. The proposals involved creating an enlarged urban authority centred on the greater Belfast area where the larger proportion of the population lives and two rural agencies covering the rest of the province in an approximate north-south division: in effect the removal of two of the existing Boards. An immediate campaign was launched by supporters for their survival mindful not least of the loss of employment that would accompany the re-organisation. Opposition was strongest in the west of the province where high percentages of unemployment and past political and cultural discrimination experienced by the predominantly Nationalist population combined to make a formidable case for the retention of the Board in that area which had been earmarked for dissolution.

The controversy was resolved in favour of the status quo by the strength of local opposition to the plan and pressure from Unionist MPs whose nine votes at that stage were crucial to the then (1992-97) minority Conservative government's survival. The minister responsible for the decision at the time did make it clear, however, that it was a temporary expedient and that the matter would be re-visited in the future. In this campaign the Unionists were given support from the most of the other MPs, Nationalist and other Unionists alike. In any future attempt to rationalise the administrative structure of education in Northern Ireland the government is faced with the problem of the way in which any re-organisation will be affected by demography and its political implications. The majority of Protestants live in the east and north of the country with the bulk of the population in the south and west predominantly Catholic. An east-west split would be interpreted as sectarian since the geographical split would also represent a Catholic-Protestant divide. In terms of the structure matching people's educational needs, a north-south grouping does not make much sense either since it would still need to take the greater Belfast area as a separate district and create similar problems of religious equity of representation as in the east-west arrangements.

Defenders of the Boards make much of their integrative and stabilising effects in a divided community. This argument has some validity, particularly in the south and west of the province where the Boards include elected representatives of different political and religious interests. The presence of members associated with the Council for Catholic Maintained Schools (CCMS) on all of them has also contributed to a greater understanding of mutual problems and reduced the degree to which CCMS might have been perceived as representative of a purely sectional interest. The Boards have also helped to produce a certain convergence of attitudes amongst a significant number of those involved in the administration of education in Northern Ireland. The process which has brought this about might be best described as dialogue and co-operation on specific areas of mutual interest rather than convergence of fundamental interests. It is a step in the right direction but it has not affected the general population nor even the perceptions of teachers who, Leckey (1993) reveals in a survey of school principals, have quite varying attitudes to the Boards, depending on the management sectors in which they work. Protestants are generally aware of and have more contact with the Boards than Catholic teachers who are more distanced and circumspect in their relationships.

The Voluntary Sector

In chapter one it was argued that the current denominational system of schooling is based on the wider cultural, religious and political differences evident before and after the creation of Northern Ireland and more acutely during the last 30 years of community conflict. This is not to argue that segregated schooling is the sole cause of the Troubles, past discrimination in employment and the political disempowerment of Nationalists are probably more significant reasons for the conflict. The government's policy since 1989 in providing active support for integrated schools is, however, a signal of its recognition that separate schooling is at least an impediment to better mutual understanding and tolerance of each other's culture and beliefs. At the same time, in recognising that the system is unlikely to change in the near future, the DENI has attempted to work through the schools to promote greater mutual understanding and tolerance by the introduction of the cross-curricular themes outlined earlier. At a more general level of the underpinning principles of the system, there is acceptance by the government that a voluntary sector as an expression of freedom of religious conscience made up, for the most part, of the Catholic primary and secondary schools, would continue to be a significant feature of education in Northern Ireland. The voluntary principle has been further strengthened in 1992 by the government granting full funding to those voluntary schools who wished to take it up. These chiefly Catholic schools had formerly to find 15% of any new capital costs as the *quid-pro-quo* for their semi-independence. The settlement means that the government has now achieved, in large measure, its initial aim at the time of partition of bringing the Catholic schools into the state sector. The chief distinguishing features remaining are that the schools are permitted to retain and promote a Catholic ethos and also that the Church still owns the schools. From the government's viewpoint, it now has greater representation in the management and running of the Catholic sector and can therefore more accurately account for public expenditure on all areas of schooling. The acceptance on both sides indicates a further stage of rapprochement between the DENI and the Catholic Church over the administration and ethos of the maintained schools. The end result is a system of voluntary Catholic schools in tandem with the state sector both of which are now wholly funded by the government.

The acceptance by successive governments since partition of the voluntary principle means that more than half the pupil population in Northern Ireland do not attend schools controlled by the Education and Library Boards. These non-controlled schools are of two management types: by far the larger

60

section consists of maintained schools, primary and secondary, for which the Council for Catholic Maintained Schools (CCMS) has a large measure of administrative responsibility. The Council is the employer of all teachers within its schools. In fact, it is the largest single employer of teachers in Northern Ireland although, like the Boards, it does not pay teachers' salaries. It has special responsibilities in relation to procedures for appointments, promotions and general school management. The Boards, however, also have responsibilities for these schools in respect of recurrent expenditure and building maintenance, as well as welfare and psychological services. In addition, two members of the Board of Governors of each school are nominated by the area Board. For this reason such schools in terms of the Education (Northern Ireland) Reform Order (1989) are not designated as voluntary schools. Since, however, they are owned by independent trustees and their general management is in the care of CCMS, they may be regarded as a particular manifestation of the 'voluntary principle'.

As the administrative authority for maintained sector, the Council for Catholic Maintained Schools (CCMS) is a comparative newcomer to the system. It was established as a statutory body by the Education Reform Order in 1989, though it existed in pre-legislative form some time previously. The need for such a body had been raised in the Astin Report (1979) and it was devised at a time when there was little sign of the magnitude of impending change produced by subsequent educational reform. When it came into existence formally on 1 April 1990, however, substantial management responsibilities were being devolved to governors of individual schools. CCMS was unhappy with the role given to it by the Education Reform Order which in its view reduced the functions of the Council as originally agreed between the Church authorities and government in 1987: 'Part of the authority they got should in our opinion have remained with the Council', (Former Director of CCMS: Leckey; 1993). Both sides were clear that the Council would not function as an extra Education and Library Board. A major point at issue, however, was the Council's duty to promote the effective management and control of Catholic maintained schools by their Boards and what that should entail. The first Director of the Council took the view that this responsibility had been interpreted in too restrictive a way by government. In relation to other matters such as employment of teachers the Council argued that it seemed to have been given responsibility without adequate executive control.

Despite these difficulties CCMS appears to have successfully assumed the role of an agency which services and advises its schools in matters of management. A majority of principals in maintained schools, especially at secondary level, believe that the Council will help to improve administration and management within their schools. There was also a general perception on the part of those interviewed by Leckey and of the teachers she surveyed that the existence of CCMS would be to the general benefit of the schools under its aegis. It would, however, be wrong to convey the impression that the advent of CCMS was warmly welcomed. Teachers and administrators outside the maintained sector were generally cautious in their judgements, partly, one might guess, from their lack of knowledge and partly from their perception of it as representing an interest which could detract from their own.

The Voluntary Grammar Schools

The other major element in the voluntary sector is made up of fifty four grammar schools which have a status similar in many ways to that of the Grant Maintained Schools in England and Wales established by the Education Reform Act (1988). They receive funding directly from DENI which they deal with on an individual basis and have had long experience of managing their own budgets. Many of these schools have strong religious affiliations, both Catholic (the Church owns them) and Protestant, and some of them have a significant mix of pupils from both denominations. Historically, there have been fewer grammar school places for Catholic pupils because of the capital costs needed to be derived from an already economically disadvantage community. There is also evidence of significant under-funding of Catholic schools by successive Unionist administrations; informal estimates, referred to earlier in chapter one, put this at around £20m over the period since partition although these figures have been hotly disputed by the DENI.

In the past there was some degree of 'crossover' mostly of Catholic pupils because of the fewer number of places available in Catholic grammar schools. In an area of sparse Catholic grammar school provision, for example, pupils who were entitled from their 11+ test result to a place had to attend a Protestant grammar school or face travelling long distances. More recently, the 'cross-over' effect could be attributed to wider educational opportunity and other sociological changes that have occurred over the last 30 to 40 years and accelerated by equality of employment legislation implemented by The Fair Employment Commission created under direct rule legislation. The combined effect has been greater representation of Catholic men and women in all sectors and levels of employment where formerly there had been discrimination on entry to a number of occupations and progress to senior positions. One of the outcomes over this period, as argued earlier, has been the emergence of a culturally and economically confident Catholic middle class. It is arguable that a sizeable proportion of them see the more prestigious Protestant grammar schools as the means of securing the best opportunities for their children.

Twenty-seven of the voluntary grammar schools have retained their status by choosing to remain responsible for raising 15% of any new capital costs, such as new buildings. Twenty-five have accepted 100% funding for building projects and two receive no capital funding from the government. The interests of all the grammar schools are represented by the non-statutory Governing Bodies Association. Whilst each school reserves the right to speak independently, the Association has managed to attain a substantial degree of influence on government policy where it sees the schools' interests threatened. The most obvious example of its impact occurred when the Labour government of the 1970s attempted to introduce comprehensive schools in 1977 consistent with their policy in England and Wales. The Association, in collaboration with others, was able to mobilise sufficient opposition among parents to have the policy overturned. Its success then, and the continuing strength of the schools' influence is related to the prestige associated with the grammar schools based on the high academic and social premium parents attach to securing a place for their children. It is one area of schooling where parents of both denominations are at one, as are the Churches, which also passively support the sector. One of the consequences is the informal ranking of primary schools according to their levels of success in the 11+ test much to the frustration of local headteachers. The other is the distortion of the upper primary curriculum as teachers, under pressure from parents to obtain the maximum number of 'passes' concentrate on preparing pupils for the 11+ by the administration of practice tests to the detriment of the wider curriculum.

Conclusions

So far a description of the Northern Ireland educational system has been set within a framework of the roles of government, the Education and Library Boards and other agencies chiefly voluntary in character such as the CCMS and the Governing Bodies Association. This has led to certain conclusions: the system is highly centralised; it is strongly influenced by events outside its immediate borders and; it is over-administered. Nevertheless in general terms, it is suggested here that allowing for regional variations, the Northern Ireland system conforms to the pattern which prevails in the rest of the United Kingdom. It has, however, two major distinguishing and connected features which affect interaction between its constituent elements. These are the size of the voluntary sector and the importance of religious affiliation as a factor in cultural, educational and social identification.

Because of these differences a purely structural account of the system conceived in terms of a top-down model along the lines of the English system of central and local authorities with an appendage of independent/grant-aided schools can be misleading. The plain fact is that in Northern Ireland over half the school population does not attend what might be referred to as 'state' schools. This is in striking contrast to the situation in England and Wales where the majority of pupils still attend local authority schools. In the light of this difference it is reasonable to expect that the dynamics of the Northern Ireland system will differ from those of England and Wales. The research conducted by McKeown and Leckey, quoted earlier, particularly the interviews, lends support to this view. It suggests that in terms of strategic decisions about the school system there are two main 'players'. On the one side is the state operating chiefly through the DENI and subsidiary bodies such as the Council for Curriculum Evaluation and Assessment for Northern Ireland. On the other is the voluntary sector represented by Church and voluntary school authorities. That is not to say that relationships between the two are necessarily antagonistic. There is too much interdependence in the reliance of the voluntary sector on state funding, for instance, to permit that. There is also a substantial element of interaction in terms of the Boards' responsibilities for maintained schools and the relationship between CCMS and DENI. With all these qualifications it is still arguable that to view the system in terms of this dualism helps to explain certain other of its features such as its centralist characteristics, and the restricted role, as far as policy is concerned, played by the Boards. The issue here when we talk about 'high-level' decisions, typically involving the government and the Churches and voluntary authorities, is essentially one of power.

Policy, Power and Equity

Power may be defined as the capacity to control resources so as to affect others. When this control is realised in terms of initiating or preventing change there can be no doubt that as far as education policy is concerned, power resides pre-eminently at the centre. It embraces both financial and intellectual resources and extends into such vital areas as, for example, the content and structure of the curriculum, the supply and training of teachers, as well as the structures of educational administration. Ultimately the arbiter of these matters is Parliament acting through government legislation and ministerial regulation. All of this is commonplace in most advanced democratic states. Recent legislation such as the Education Reform Act (1988) and the Education Reform (Northern Ireland) Order (1989) exemplify it. Indeed, they do so to such an extent as to raise doubt about any proposal which assigns a major role to other agencies or interests.

In relation specifically to the voluntary sector, however, it must be noted that its representatives, either administrators or headteachers, do not perceive themselves as yielding anything more than a modest influence. CCMS was bitterly disappointed at the role given to it in the 1989 Order. The Catholic bishops failed in their case when they went to judicial review in 1990 over the government's decision to fund grant maintained religiously integrated schools to the extent of 100% finance on capital costs while the Catholic maintained sector continued to receive 15% less, but were subsequently successful in obtaining funding in full for their schools in 1992. In what sense then can it be meaningful to talk about power in connection with the voluntary sector? The most obvious meaning is negative control: the capacity to prevent something happening. An example is the effective opposition mounted by the Catholic Church to the implementation of the interim report of the Chilver Committee in 1982 which established the University of Ulster and recommended the amalgamation of the two Catholic and one Protestant (officially non-denominational) colleges of education. In the eyes of the Catholic Church its proposals would have diminished the status of the Catholic teacher-training colleges to an unacceptable level. Other voices, perhaps notably Presbyterian in support of the Protestant college oficially non-denominational, were raised in opposition but there can be little doubt that it was the strong objections of the Catholics which stayed the government's hand. The Chilver episode illustrates another aspect of negative control. It is episodic in the sense that it is most likely to be effective in the context of wider social and political events. In the case of Chilver this wider context was important. At the time of the report the political scene in Northern Ireland had been agitated by the deaths of hunger-strikers and general problems of security. In such circumstances it would have seemed foolhardy for government to risk provoking a large section of the minority community.

Another example of the exercise of power affected by wider factors was the announcement in November 1992 of an accommodation between Church and state in relation to the funding of schools under maintained status. It is now possible for such schools to apply for 100% funding in return for a change in the post-Astin provisions whereby the trustees, (representing the Church authorities who own the schools), will surrender the majority of the members whom they nominate to boards of Governors. Similar arrangements are available to other schools such as voluntary grammar schools which up to now have received 85% grant-aid for capital projects. It is likely that a significant part of the background to this arrangement was the judicial review sought by the Catholic bishops in 1990 and the publication, somewhat delayed by criticisms from DENI which disputed the findings, of the report outlined earlier, by the Standing Advisory Commission on Human Rights in 1991 concerning the under-funding of Catholic schools.

To its credit the government had been striving for a number of years to abolish structural inequalities between the two communities in Northern Ireland. It could not refuse to act in such circumstances, even if it were so minded, and it chose to do so in a way which further fastened the maintained sector to the general state apparatus of educational administration. In this instance, concessions were traded by both sides and it is arguable that the government got a good bargain. Since 1930 successive Stormont Unionist administrations tried to bring the Catholic sector into closer relationship with rest of the state provided system. No significant move occurred until the early seventies when the Church authorities accepted two public representatives (in the case of the Catholic maintained schools two nominated by the Boards) on boards of governors. The establishment of CCMS as a statutory body was a further move in the same direction. The new arrangements which will provide 100% grant for both capital and recurrent expenditure might be regarded as an almost inevitable convergence. There were of course other factors, not least of which have been the financial pressures on the maintained sector arising from educational reform, particularly in the provision of science and technology. Another contributing reason may be found in the existence of the Grant Maintained Integrated schools (GMIS) which have similar funding arrangements. Most important, however, was something referred to by a former education minister, Jeremy Hanley, in his comment on the introduction of this new form of maintained school funding:

> The most important message in these new arrangements is that all concerned in the running of voluntary schools-the trustees of the schools and the public

authorities-recognise that they have sufficient confidence in one another to be able to trust in this sort of partnership. (1993)

It is arguable that this trust has something to do with the existence of direct rule.

Two final points may be made. Firstly, the government has managed the Northern Ireland system in such away as to accommodate diversity of management status, with the cultural and political dimensions that this entails, within what is now a unified administrative framework. It is clear also that the consequences of the 1989 Education Reform Order in Northern Ireland go beyond the administrative and educational structures provided in the legislation. Indeed, they raise the question as to what extent hard and fast distinctions can be made between so-called state and non-state schools in any but a fairly minimal way. In so far as any distinction may be maintained it relates more to cultural, political and social factors rather than educational provision. It might be equally meaningful to speak of different kinds of state schools.

Secondly, educational policy-making in Northern Ireland is conducted against a background on which national and local politics impinge in a unique way. The latter in particular may act as brake on the rate of change. Nevertheless, it must be said that immediately before the onset of the education reforms in 1989 the system showed a considerable capacity for innovation in programmes such as the Guidelines for Primary Schools and the 11 to 16 project for secondary schools. It has also coped well, although with considerable strain for its teachers, with educational reform. If ability to adapt is a necessary condition for survival the system's vital signs appear to be strong enough.

Finally, the Catholic Church's ability to engage in such bargaining depends to some extent on its moral position derived from its religious authority. It relies to a much greater degree, however, on its support from the Catholic section of the population as the guarantor of its cultural aspirations and identity through ownership of the schools and the protection of their Catholic ethos. Much of this stems from the way in which past political and economic structures discriminated against Catholics. With employment pathways closed in significant ways and the absence of Nationalist culture and symbols in the official presentation of civil society in Northern Ireland, education and in particular Catholic grammar schools, became the chief dynamic for realising social and economic equality. The Catholic Church authorities because of their central role in providing the schools and their representation of wider social and cultural values, have been able to act, in certain circumstances, as an equal 'power-broker' with the government in determining educational policy.

4 Policy in Practice

Selection at Eleven: The Retention of the 11+

In the previous section it was argued that the power of the Churches has often been exercised in a negative way; that is, they have more often argued against and significantly amended central government's educational policies according to their perceived denominational and cultural needs. The segregated pattern of schooling in Northern Ireland is a reflection of those differences. Cathcart (1990) argues that:

> The history of British educational legislation as applied to Northern Ireland is revealing for it enables us to establish how British educational policy was reshaped in the province as a means of maintaining two distinct cultures. (P.3)

Nowhere is this more evident than in the continuing presence of selection at eleven for a highly prized place at a grammar school. The alternative is a non-selective secondary intermediate school for the greater number of children who do not 'pass' the 11+ examination. Whilst selection remains a vestigial aspect of educational policy in a small number of LEAs in England and Wales, it has been retained as the underlying principle of the province's system of secondary education. There is some evidence, however, that new forms of selection are occurring in England with regard to City Technological Colleges and the more popular Grant Maintained Schools. All the CTCs, for instance, are over-subscribed and are forced to select pupils from those who apply. The schools are not permitted to use academic criteria and rely on their estimates of the pupils'and parents' commitment and motivation based on their application and, crucially, an interview with pupils and parents. They have to be willing also to pay any transport costs and have shorter holidays because of the introduction of a four term year. Walford (1992) provides evidence about the effects of this form of creaming on local comprehensive schools:

> ...heads and teachers in the nearby LEA schools claimed that the CTC was selecting those very parents who have the most interest in their children's education, and those children who are most keen and enthusiastic. They argue that the CTC was selecting children who, while they might not be particularly

academically able, were seen as invigorating the atmosphere of any school, providing models for other children, and being the most rewarding for teachers to teach. (P. 97)

The Conservative government of 1992-97 instituted a policy debate aimed at assessing the likely response among parents towards the re-introduction of selection with the suggestion of establishing one grammar school in every town or where parents wished it. The reaction among the bulk of parents was muted in the realisation that one grammar school meant several secondary moderns nearby and they were decidedly unenthusiastic about bringing back the trauma of selection. The new Labour administration has adopted a policy of 'let sleeping dogs lie' in acceding to the presence of grammar schools where they have survived the 1960s and 70s policy of going comprehensive.

The Scots, by contrast, stand out as the area of the United Kingdom where comprehensive schooling is the normal pattern for almost all their schools. In Northern Ireland, the area, covering Craigavon, Portadown and Lurgan and accounting for approximately 10% of the age group, is the only part of Northern Ireland which has adopted a system of comprehensive provision consisting of junior high schools from 11 to 14 years and senior highs for 14 to 16 years. On the basis of the pupil's performance at age 14, a recommendation is made for a place at either a selective grammar school type or a non-selective secondary senior high school to prepare, respectively, for a curriculum aimed at achieving three A levels and higher education or, alternatively, ending with GCSEs, NVQs and the labour market, a government training programme or the newly introduced 'Welfare to Work' scheme. Elsewhere in Northern Ireland there are a small number of schools officially designated as comprehensive schools where pupils from neaby primary schools transfer automatically. Parents can, if they wish, ask for their children to take the 11+ and, in the context of open enrolment, send them to the nearest grammar school.

From the beginning of free secondary education for everyone in Northern Ireland, the power of the voluntary bodies discussed in chapter three was a major factor in reshaping the intentions and the framing of the province's equivalent of the Butler Education Act passed in Great Britain in 1944. The parallel legislation was introduced to Northern Ireland in 1947. The Governing Bodies Association, formed at the time to protect the grammar schools' interests, argued successfully that they should retain more of their traditional rights to chose pupils than was allowed for in the British legislation. In this they effectively applied to be treated in the same way as the direct grant schools and for a very small number as quasi-public schools. The outcome was that, in return for 65% of capital grants and full recurrent funding on a per-capita basis, paid directly from the DENI, most of the schools in the voluntary grammar sector agreed to allocate 80% of their places to pupils who had an academic 'aptitude' as indicated by the selection test. They were successful in avoiding any formal control or management relationship with the local county education committees. A small group of richer and academically prestigious schools gave no such guarantee and accepted no capital grants reserving, in effect, the right to chose whoever they wished. In official terms, and contrary to the position in Great Britain, pupils were awarded scholarships for attendance at all the grammar schools to be paid for by the DENI directly to the school, a figure which varied according to the amount that it had traditionally charged. This concession, revealed only 40 years later, (Cathcart; 1990), had the effect of rendering a scholarship at one of the partially opted out schools, some of which affected public school status, costing four times as much as one in a neighbouring school accepting capital grants. The grammar schools, in addition, were then and remain entitled to charge 'top-up' capital fees. In more recent times these have been capped according to an upper limit set by the DENI. The difference in fees was also meant to take into account the higher costs of upkeep and maintenance of the extensive grounds and playing fields of some of the grammar schools.

This did two things: it rescued a large proportion of grammar schools from years of poverty, and under-funding. It also undermined central government's intention to provide grammar school places for all who were academically able irrespective of their ability to afford it. This had the effect of reducing the total number of places available through giving the schools discretion over 20% of their intake. In practice, it provided for mostly middle class parents, who could afford it, a means of obtaining a grammar school place in the event of their child being an 'unqualified' pupil having 'failed' the test. These arrangements were contrary to the spirit of the 1944 Act and the practice in Great Britain, where places in public sector schools were confined to those who had 'passed' the 11+. The quotas at the time did not include boarders and it still remains possible for a parent whose child has been unsuccessful in the test to obtain a grammar school place by paying boarding fees at a number of schools still offering such places, ostensibly for overseas pupils. In addition, many of the grammar schools have held on to their preparatory departments even in the case of those that have transferred into the state system.

In the event of a poor result in the selection test, it was claimed that, in the past, unsuccessful preparatory school pupils were given preferential

71

treatment through manipulation of the review procedure. A child in this position was taken into the grammar school as a fee payer and then after age 12, usually in the second year, on the basis of the head's estimation that the pupil could match the attainment of the qualifiers, he or she was granted a scholarship. The process was also open to pupils in secondary intermediate and unre-organised primary schools which continued for some time in their former mode as public elementary schools taking pupils up to the school leaving age of 15. The bias, it was argued, lay in the greater ease of transition of borderline preparatory school pupils to a non-fee paying place in the grammar school: they tended to be seen by the senior school as the junior part of the larger school. A secondary pupil had the added barrier of the school not wishing to lose an able child and the fact of moving to a new school with the accompanying personal adjustments of making new friends often from different social class backgrounds. There were also the considerable financial costs of uniforms, capital fees or extra travel.

Something of a historical anomaly remains in regard to the funding of the preparatory schools which is somewhat different from their wholly independent equivalents in Great Britain. At present, parents' fees are subsidised to the tune of about £1.5m from the DENI which, in a region with high levels of social disadvantage, appears somewhat generous to mostly middle class parents: doubly so, since the departments are all attached to Protestant grammar schools. The family on a low income may not see this as a wise or equitable use of public funds drawn however meagrely or indirectly from their taxes. The amount given to the schools by the DENI has been construed as a subsidy for middle class Protestants (McGill;1996a), in contrast to parents elsewhere in the United Kingdom who would expect to pay the full cost of private education for their children. The argument in their favour is that they save the state system money by partially removing the cost of educating preparatory school pupils who would otherwise attend public sector schools. The current subsidy would therefore be replaced, the argument goes, by a much larger sum needed to fund state school places. This viewpoint is obviated by the number of surplus places in state schools.

Proponents of the grammar school sector argue that, in granting the schools control of over 20% of grammar school places, the Ministry of Education at the time prevented the development of independent schools charging fees outside the means of the greater majority of people. Its greater effect, however, was to reduce further the availability of grammar school places. The absence of a significant independent sector is still used today as an argument in support of the grammar schools and contributed to their ability to retain fee-paying and the control of places, allowed in 1947, until as late as 1990 when scholarships were abolished as part of the Education Reform Order. The technical secondary schools, which were intended to form the third part of the tri-partite arrangements, failed to realise their potential not least because of their delayed entry at age 13, but also opposition from the Local Education Committees which wanted to protect their secondary intermediate schools. The scale of the building programme needed to construct the new secondary intermediate system meant that many pupils who were supposed to attend the non-selective secondaries, on the basis of 11+, remained in what were officially described as unre-orginised primary schools. The 'techs', as they were known, were discontinued in 1964 with the result that, as in Great Britain, the system became a bi-partite one with the grammar schools and the secondary intermediates the chief components of the Northern Ireland secondary sector. The rate of growth of the latter can be seen by the number of enrolments in 1950 when two-thirds of post-primary pupils were in grammar schools. By 1975 the reverse was the case: the building programme for secondary schools had progressed to the extent that the majority of pupils were now attending purpose built secondary schools as the Act had intended. Currently, a conservative estimate of grammar schools' intake across the whole of the sector would be around 40% of post-primary sector enrolments. This is somewhat higher than the official figure of 35% but it is an indication of a significant degree of permeability in terms of entrance criteria when considering that they were originally thought to be suitable only for the top 25-27%. The higher figure also reflects some grammar schools' need to admit pupils with lower 11+ grades in order to fill their quotas, usually in areas of over provision of places.

Initially, selection was determined by an attainment test consisting in Northern Ireland of English composition, English language, arithmetic and an intelligence test used mostly in border line cases. This pattern was amended during the 1950s and 60s by reducing the volume of attainment assessment in arithmetic and English and increasing the importance of the intelligence testing part of the procedure by the introduction of two IQ papers. In 1961, for example, a pupil obtaining an IQ result of more than 130 was automatically qualified irrespective of marks obtained in the English and arithmetic examinations. In 1966, the procedure was streamlined further by the replacement of English and arithmetic by two intelligence tests augmented by teachers' assessments of the pupils' attainment in the normal school subjects. On this basis teachers ranked their pupils' suitability for grammar school. This reform and parents' increased ambitions for their children had the effect of greatly boosting the number of children entered for the test from 54% of the age group in 1950 to 95% in 1970 (Wilson;1987)

Criticism of selection took two forms: that it was wrong in principle and; that the testing procedure was at fault. The argument on principle was stated clearly by the government's Advisory Council for Education in its report of 1973 recommending the discontinuation of selection, initially it advised, by a statement of intent to this effect from the minister responsible. The government's intentions were realised in 1977 when the Minister of State, Lord Melchett, established a working group:

> to consider an alternative to the existing 11+ Selection Procedure for transfer into secondary education, for adoption in an interim period while the reorganisation of secondary education is under consideration.

By this time, direct rule had been operating for five years under a Labour government which was already expressing some disquiet, as expressed by the Prime Minister James Callaghan in his Ruskin speech of 1976, about the direction and quality of learning delivered by the education system in England. The perception of many people, especially supporters of the Northern Ireland grammar schools, was that this was a policy being imposed from outside on a successful system at a time when the prime minister James Callaghan was expressing publicly government reservations about the quality and standards of the largely comprehensive system in England and Wales. In defending the grammar schools, local politicians, concerned parents and the Governing Bodies Association pointed to their pupils' success in achieving the best A level results in the United Kingdom. The figures for Northern Ireland boys and girls achieving three or more A levels in 1992 were respectively 20% and 25%. The results for England and Wales were boys:17% and girls:18%, (NIEC;1995).

These data need to be interpreted carefully in relation to the lower number of pupils entered for public examinations in Northern Ireland. The pattern of results at A level is to some extent a result of 'creaming', which in practice means that, compared with Great Britain, a narrower and more able band of pupils is entered for the examinations. Its corollary is a greater number becoming alienated from school work with the result that Northern Ireland has the greatest proportion of pupils in the United Kingdom leaving with poor or without any qualifications. This aspect of the system's performance was not widely known during the 1960s and 70s and only became evident during the 1980s when 28% of boys and 19% of girls in Northern Ireland were leaving without qualifications. The comparable figures for England and Wales were boys 12% and girls 9% (Daly; 1987).

The pattern of low attainment for the majority of school leavers is not confined to Northern Ireland with the overall United Kingdom's figures comparing unfavourably with other countries in Europe and elsewhere. In Germany and France, for example, over 60% of 16 year olds in 1994 left with the equivalent of GCSE grades of A-C in maths, the national language and one science, compared with 27% in England and Northern Ireland (22%). (NIEC; 1995. P.35). Over the longer term the schools' record shows one of improvement when comparing those leaving with one or more A levels: in 1963-64 there were 1500 (8%) rising to 6,500 (32%) who left with the qualification in 1992-93. The respective figures for pupils leaving without passing the equivalent of one O level or a grade C or better at GCSE in the same years are 18,000 (77%) in 1963-64 and 5,000 (25%) in 1992-93, (Gallagher; 1996).

The improvement in attainment figures needs also to be qualified in the context of the raising of the school leaving age in 1972 giving pupils more opportunity and receiving more encouragement from teachers to take a public examination in order to improve their performance and vocational prospects as well as their schools' academic reputation. This was especially the case as enrolments began to fall from the late 1970s onwards when schools found themselves having to compete for pupils. The independent control of their budgets granted in 1989 also meant that funding was effectively awarded on a per-pupil basis. That had a further upward 'ratcheting' effect on the pressure for schools to produce good results in order to sustain enrolments if they were to avoid making teachers redundant, or in the case of some, having to close because of decreasing pupil numbers. McKeown in a survey for the DENI on the effects of giving schools control of their budgets found that there is now an educational market within the Catholic and Protestant post-primary sectors:

> More than three quarters of schools…believed themselves to face direct competition from other schools for pupils…there is evidence of competition between grammar and secondary schools, especially in localities in which pupil numbers are declining. In such competition grammar schools have an inbuilt advantage with respect to student enrolment. In localities where pupil numbers are declining, or in which grammar school places were over-provided, grammar schools have been obliged to admit some pupils who have not achieved higher grades in the Transfer Procedure…Perhaps arising from this, some secondary school principals indicated that they were being asked to admit into years 10 and 11 a number of pupils from grammar schools. (DENI; 1997. P.7)

There has also been the more general increase in credentialism where increasing competition for jobs has lead to inflation in the level of qualification demanded by employers and has made pupils more conscious of the need for GCSE, A level passes, and the different types of NVQ courses. An added difficulty for the non-selective secondaries came with the introduction of open enrolment as part of the 1989 Reform Order. Within the province's selective system, parents' freedom of choice has inevitably favoured the grammar schools whilst simultaneously destabilising further the enrolments of many of the secondaries which are forced to compete for pupils with the selective schools in a competition weighted against them by the academic creaming effects of the 11+. The degree of structural insecurity produced by selection can be seen from a survey by McKeown and colleagues in 1996 which found in 1994-95 that 93% of grammar schools had taken up between 95 and 100% of their enrolment capacity compared with only 34% of secondary schools. In addition, 30% of secondary schools were only three quarters full in contrast to 2% of grammar schools. Overall, pupil numbers in a fifth of secondaries had fallen since 1992 by an average of 10% in contrast with little change over the period in the grammar sector. Whilst there is little information on the implications of this degree of variability for staffing, distribution of resources and coverage of the curriculum, it is arguable that there are problems for a number of secondary schools in these areas directly related to the run-on effects of selection. In terms of effective use of public finance, it provides further insight into the apparent anomaly of higher global spending on education in Northern Ireland compared with Great Britain, whilst less is spent at the level of individual pupils.

In attempting to achieve a balanced intake of pupils with regard to their ability, secondary schools are hampered by the rules imposed by DENI on both types of schools in the criteria for entry which they can publish in the schools' prospectuses. The grammar schools can include academic criteria indicating to parents the likely pace and depth of learning offered, while the secondary schools are prevented from including any higher order intellectual entry requirements in prospective pupils. In addition, only the grammar schools are allowed to use the results of the 11+ in deciding whether or not to accept a pupil. The net effect has been an increase in grammar school enrolments to the extent that a very conservative estimate would suggest they are attracting approximately 40% of enrolments rather than the originally intended most able quarter of the age group. There would also be regional variations in districts with surplus places, where schools would take more than the notional 40%. This percentage includes successful secondary school pupils, who had

76

originally 'failed', transferring into the grammar schools' sixth forms on the basis of good GCSEs and is another indication of the limitations on the predictive accuracy of the current 11+. It questions the educational value of imposing this type of 'high stakes' test at such an early stage of children's development when their later progress and attainment shows the original result and prediction to be incorrect. Gallagher (1988) provides evidence that about one in six pupils are wrongly placed on the basis of their 11+ result when attainment is measured at 16+. He shows that 67% of the M or intermediate grade at the time (1988-94), and 16% of 'unqualified' pupils achieved passes in four or more O levels. In another study, Sutherland (1993) concludes:

> the percentage who appear misplaced will be 20%…a substantial percentage of misplacements therefore seems inevitable in selection…How serious this is depends partly on the consequence of selection…By the time of the 1981 cohort studies, secondary intermediate pupils might sit public examinations but they performed less well than those with a similar score or grade at 11+ who were enrolled in grammar schools…the curriculum for M (middle) grade pupils in grammar and secondary became increasingly differentiated. (P.111)

The fact that some of the larger more successful secondary schools have also established small sixth forms offering a limited number of A level subjects for their own pupils, underscores doubts about academic projections made at 11 from the results of the transfer test. Officially, the schools are discouraged in this policy on the reasonable grounds of efficient use of resources and teachers' time for what are often very small classes. The schools have persisted, however, not least because of its value as the school's academic 'flagship' when persuading parents to enrol their children. The DENI appears to have adopted a passive policy of bi-lateralism in post-primary schooling hoping in some way that the common curriculum will confer parity of esteem between the two types of school: a system of non-selective 11 to 16 and selective 11 to 18 schools running in parallel. The grammar schools, not unnaturally, are happy to comply with such a development and pleased to accept able pupils to their sixth forms and have made transfer at 16 a relatively easy process. There still remains a certain contradiction in any future development of such a policy in so far as academic creaming at age 11 will continue to the disadvantage of the secondary intermediate schools in terms of their restricted academic intake and the deterrent effect on parents' choices of non-selective schools. The continuation of selection in Northern Ireland, confirmed in DENI's 'Learning for Life', has been attenuated somewhat by the new Labour education minister's recent announcement that, in line with policy in England and Wales, parents can, if they wish, opt for comprehensive schools. Whilst not doubting the minister's personal commitment to achieving equality of opportunity through comprehensive education, the inbuilt advantages of the grammar school sector render his offer of providing such schools a somewhat empty one.

Selection was abandoned in England and Wales in large measure because of middle class parents' dissatisfaction with the variability and, in politically significant areas, the scarcity of grammar school places. Similar parents in Northern Ireland are only too pleased with the current high levels of access to grammar schools, with the result that there has been no significant or politically articulate lobby for comprehensive education. Dissatisfaction is concentrated on the form of the selection process and whether or not it is as fair as it can be. From the government's viewpoint, there appears to be no immediate pressure to introduce comprehensive-type education. Such is the premium set by parents on a grammar school place, that the sector is at present capable of tolerating high levels of variability of pupils' ability on intake as measured by the 11+. This is also true of differences in the academic success of individual grammar schools as measured by their GCSE and A level results. Some grammar schools, for instance, because of locality or reputation, are able to fill their intake quotas entirely with pupils gaining an A grade in the 11+. Others for similar reasons have to include pupils with Bs and Cs in order to complete their quotas. The latter schools are able to shelter beneath the umbrella of the sector's prestige and its perceived overall academic success.

Future policy with respect to the presentation of schools' examination results in parallel with an added value index showing contributory factors such as ability of intake, levels of disadvantage, gender, and so on will give a more accurate picture of a school's effectiveness. It may well be that the annual examination league tables will require substantial re-interpretation. Some secondary schools, for instance, may be performing better than their raw results would suggest when their catchment circumstances are taken into account as expressed by an added value index. The converse might be true of some outwardly successful counterparts in the grammar sector which might be under-performing when their results are weighed in the context of an added value index taking into account the quality of intake and catchment area.

In relation to the increasing volume and variability of grammar school enrolments two conclusions can be drawn. First, a number of grammar schools, especially at the lower end of the performance league ratings and parents' ranking of social and academic prestige, now have an increasing but still small comprehensive ability intake. McKeown (1997), for example, found: 'evidence that the publication of entry grades for post-primary schools

78

has resulted in volatility in the number and quality of applications for year eight placement in grammar schools' (McKeown et al; 1997. P.7). It is unclear whether or not teachers in this position have adopted different teaching styles more suited to that section of their pupils who are at the middle and lower ends of the ability range. There is no evidence either at school or system level of any inservice training to this effect, leading to the observation that such schools are reluctant to admit that such a problem exists. It seems also probable that a proportion of pupils of modest ability in such grammar schools are academically 'in at the deep end'. McKeown, whose work was quoted earlier, found in fact that some were transferred into the non-selective schools. Teachers who have been used to high ability pupils' faster pace of learning cannot be expected to adapt to the needs of slower paced learners without some guidance about the different skills required.

The second inference is that open enrolment has effectively top-sliced the ability range of the secondary schools by drawing off the middle range pupils who formerly came to them but whose parents are now able to chose and obtain a place in a selective school. This has been caused by the increasing availability of grammar places as a result of the more general fall in numbers of the age group, leaving some schools with empty places to fill. The fact that the outcome of selection is no longer presented as an absolute pass or fail but as a six point scale has introduced further discretion in the choice of pupils accepted by the grammar schools. Currently, an 11 year old's result in the test is given in descending order as one of the following A, B1, B2, C1, C2, or D. An A grade guarantees a grammar school place, a pupil with a B1 will normally obtain one but location has an important bearing since grammar schools are not evenly spread across the province. The segregated nature of the schools means, for example, that in some areas there is a relative scarcity of Catholic grammar schools and in others more Protestant pupils than available places. This has led to a number of secondary schools, for the most part Catholic, attracting increasing numbers of qualified pupils to the extent that parents now need to put them as their first choice, in preference to the grammar school, if they are to have any chance of their child being accepted. However, where there is a surfeit of grammar schools of either type, some grammar schools will tend also to take pupils with a B2 grade and in some cases C1s. The DENI, in order to prevent this type of 'mission drift' and also to protect the secondaries has imposed quotas on the grammar school intakes. The number of pupils is determined by the physical capacity of the school to accommodate them. Schools which go over their prescribed enrolment must make out a strong case for the extra pupils or risk DENI refusing to pay for them.

The secondary schools face further competition from the integrated schools which currently take approximately 3% of the age group, but continue to grow. Whilst parents know that they are not grammar schools, there is nevertheless a general perception of them as having a higher status than the non-selective secondaries, with the result that they are increasingly popular with parents. This is not to gainsay the genuinely ecumenical and altruistic motives of such parents, but the perceived intermediary academic and social status of the integrated schools with respect to selection and the background of pupils, remains a factor in many parents' reasons for choosing them for their children.

Official ambivalence towards the academic status of the integrated schools has recently been demonstrated by the DENI giving permission to one of the schools to set up a separate grammar stream. This breaches a strict interpretation of the entrance criteria since integrated schools are officially defined as non-selective secondary schools. The school successfully argued that, since it was attracting children of all ability, it should be allowed to confirm this by recruiting a comprehensive intake. In addition, the uneven geographical distribution of grammar schools led to the establishment of a small number of partially selective secondaries officially permitted to take a set proportion of qualifiers. Historically there have also been fewer grammar places available for Catholic than Protestant children. Livingstone writing in the mid-eighties found that, of pupils with the highest 11+plus grade of A, 9% of Catholic children were in non-selective schools compared with 2% of Protestants. The imbalance applied also to middle ability pupils: 20% of Catholic and 11% of Protestant M grade pupils' parents chose secondary schools. Livingstone (1987). The position is partially explained by the greater number of fee-paying places then available in Protestant grammar schools and the greater ability of Protestant parents to afford them given the strong link between religion and social class with Protestants making up the larger proportion of the middle class. Current projections suggest that by the year 2000 there will be respectively, 27,100 and 33,000 places respectively in the Catholic and Protestant grammar school sectors. (NIEC;1995. P.9). The discrepancy is ameliorated by a small but increasing proportion of middle class Catholics' preference for integrated and Protestant grammar schools for their children. The percentage in 1990 was 4.5% and in 1993, 6.3%, providing evidence of the earlier point about the emergence of an identifiable and educationally secular Catholic middle class.

Criticism of selection is also focused on the test itself which has undergone a number of changes reflecting mostly parental and schools' dissatisfaction. Recent reforms of the process have come full circle in returning to the format of the earlier tests. Two tests consisting of maths, English and science, taken in the first term of year seven. Except for science, this pattern mirrors the test structure used until 1966 and is in reality a measure of attainment and, as far as the primary schools are concerned, an assessment of their academic performance. In this respect, the test has distorted the curriculum of the upper primary school in the extent to which teaching the three subjects is subsumed as part of the preparation for the 11+. Whilst there is little recorded evidence about science, teachers complain generally of having to teach the subject as 'received wisdom' in the last two years of primary school with decreasing emphasis on experimentation and more on passive note-taking and demonstration. Research by the Northern Ireland Council for Educational Research (Sutherland; 1990) provides evidence of substantial preparation for the test with almost two thirds of principals in their sample of 199 schools reporting that preparation for the test affected the school's work to a significant extent. As a consequence other subjects such as history, geography, art and music were to some extent neglected.

Another more in-depth aspect of their research concentrated on 16 primary schools, eight in selective and eight in non-selective areas. It reveals the persistence of what the author refers to as the elementary tradition in the central emphasis in the primary curriculum of the basics of English, maths (and since the Reform Order, science), of which the better part of the tradition would be well-structured whole-class teaching. Teachers, it was concluded, see this as the best preparation for the transfer test which also fits with recent changes to the test making it an assessment of attainment in these subjects. For many primary schools their transfer results are increasingly interpreted by parents as a more direct and narrowly instrumental assessment of the quality of a school's teaching of English, maths and science. The effect is to blinker intellectually the teaching of the subjects as they become more tightly bound to achieving 'passes'. A similar hierarchy is applied to the secondary and grammar schools with respect to the number of As in the transfer test that a particular school attracts in the case of a selective school. A similar hierarchy exists within the secondary intermediate sector where, at the top end, a number of schools attract pupils with higher grades in the 11+. At the other end, there are a group of schools with intakes of predominantly low ability pupils as measured by the 11+ test.

In summary, the government's formal support of selection, whilst remaining ambivalent to the extent of 'mission drift' with respect to grammar schools' acceptance of pupils with middle and lower transfer grades on the one hand, and the growth of secondary sixth forms on the other, has a number of consequences with regard to what is now an educational market. First, parents, in seeking the best school for their children, will inevitably draw distinctions between schools. There is nothing new in this other than the more recent government imposed competitive position of schools, heightened further by falling rolls, which has lead to much sharper and publicly displayed differentiation between schools. This is especially so in the case of schools in areas of social and economic disadvantage many of whose pupils suffer all the academic, social and behavioural handicaps caused by such a background. Current policy on selection allied with open enrolment will effectively worsen the position of pupils in such schools by depriving them of any semblance of a balanced intake through more extensive academic creaming by grammar schools and better placed secondaries. It will also have the educational effect of concentrating in a small number of schools unacceptably high rates of failure in terms of pupils leaving with poor qualifications. Gallagher (1996) in his evidence to the House of Commons Northern Ireland Select Committee pointed out that government-set national attainment targets of 85% of pupils achieving five or more GCSEs at level C or NVQ three were being met by only five secondary schools. Breaking down the figures further, he reported that there was wide variation in the performance of individual schools: in some, 62% obtained this level but remained 40 secondary schools with over half their pupils failing to achieve the equivalent of one GCSE at C after twelve years of schooling. The latter schools suffer a combination of disadvantage and selection leaving the pupils with little prospects or incentive to achieve qualifications for employment. The Northern Ireland Economic Council in a survey of achievement in the province gives a bleak picture of the conditions facing such schools and their pupils:

> There is a clear and measurable link between educational achievement and social disadvantage. This may be exacerbated by a social and spatial differentiation between grammar and secondary schools. Thus, it would appear that the intakes of grammar and secondary schools differ in terms of their social class profiles, and that they differ in respect to their area of residence. The net effect is that the lowest level of achievement is found among young people in situations of multiple disadvantage...they are most likely to live in socially disadvantage areas...and attend secondary schools where many of their peers share the same background. (NIEC 1997; P.91-92)

On present analysis, the original aims of creating a more egalitarian educational system through matching ability with different types of school on the results of the 11+ appear to be frustrated for large numbers of children from working class backgrounds. It seems also to offer few prospects for pupils from families suffering long-term unemployment and other forms of disadvantage. The process may in fact make their position worse by concentrating in too many secondary schools the debilitating educational effects of selection and disadvantage. The result in many cases is a culture of low expectations and antipathy among pupils towards achievement. McGill (1996b) in his evidence to the Northern Ireland Select Committee argues that the system as a whole has successively reduced the number of pupils leaving without any qualifications. Recent changes in the selection procedure, he argues, from a verbal reasoning test to what is now an assessment of attainment in maths, English and science, will compound further the educational handicaps of disadvantaged pupils and may adversely affect their improving performance.

In June 1996, a DENI statistical circular, (Sb1/96), showed clearly that children from more prosperous families are far more likely to get a top grade (A) in the 11+ selection tests than poorer pupils. Over the last three years this gap has widened alarmingly because of the switch from verbal reasoning to attainment tests. In 1995-96, 52% of pupils in the most prosperous schools got grade A, compared with only 16% in the most deprived schools. Catholic pupils' performance in the 11+ has declined in the last three years. A key indicator, in this respect, is the proportion of free school meals taken by pupils' Contextual ...school-level variables, such as the percentage of pupils per school eligible for free school meals, also appear to be significant determinants of educational outcomes...which are compounded by the effects of neighbourhood socio-economic status' (NIEC;1997. P.66).

Despite evidence of the divisive effects of selection, DENI's policy choices appear limited by the popularity and prestige of the grammar schools. The strength of their position is such that under-achieving schools and those admitting pupils with middle and low 11+ results are able to protect their status under the general umbrella of the grammar school label. Whilst preparing for the 11+ test creates pressure for schools and stress among pupils, a grammar school place remains the central aim for parents who are naturally anxious to provide the best preparation for their children's future. As argued earlier, there is sufficient access to grammar schools for this to be a realisable aim for enough parents to sustain the system unlike the situation in England and Wales in the 1960s where the number of places varied from 35% to 10% according to where you lived. In Great Britain the abolition of selection was greatly assisted by the contribution of articulate affluent parents many of whom lived in areas of low access to grammar schools and therefore had a direct interest and involvement in reforming the system of secondary schools.

Credentialism, fuelled by changes in the pattern of qualifications needed for employment had, in addition, rendered obsolete the original policy underpinning the purpose of the secondary modern schools. In the immediate post 1944 period it was thought that they did not necessarily have to concern themselves with examinations since most of the pupils would be in routine work requiring minimal on-the-job training. The level of access to selective schools for similar middle class parents in Northern Ireland is such that sufficient numbers are able to secure grammar school places for their children and are therefore content with the present structure of secondary schooling.

Alternatives to Selection at 11

There are, however, two examples of comprehensive schooling close at hand which provide evidence that, contrary to arguments by the grammar school lobby, abandoning selection need not mean lowering standards. Non-selective schooling can in fact also go some way to improving the circumstances of those children whose education is blighted by the disadvantages of their background and its effects on their schools. The first is the system, referred to earlier, of junior and senior schools in the Craigavon area covering approximately 10% of the age group. There is no selection test at age 11 when all pupils transfer to local junior high schools for two years after which, on the basis of their progress in the previous two years, they go either to a grammar or a secondary type of high school. Wilson (1985) offers the best insights into the strengths and weaknesses of this alternative to the system's wider selective arrangements by first showing that a pupil's performance in the first year of secondary school is a more accurate indicator of later progress at 16+ than the 11+ test. Contrary to the argument of falling standards in comprehensive schools, at 18+ the Craigavon pupils were on equal footing with other Northern Ireland pupils' results. With regard to the social divisions entailed in selection, he found that socio-economic status was less obvious among pupils in the two-tier comprehensives than in the rest of the system. Social class differences were also less important as a factor influencing pupils' academic performance compared to pupils selected elsewhere in Northern Ireland at 11.

The second example concerns the experience of Scottish schools going comprehensive from 1970 to 1974. Extensive research has been conducted by Wilms and McPherson (1997) on the outcomes of abandoning selection and the introduction of what has become a predominantly 11 to 18 comprehensive system. They provide data on three groups of pupils in the first stages of the change in school organisation using the Scottish School Leavers Surveys of 1977, 1981 and 1985 for the base data. The research shows the relationship between three measures: socio-economic status (SES), attainment in the Scottish Certificate of Education (SCE) and social class. Their findings show a marked decrease in the degree of school segregation according to the ability of their intakes, which contrasts sharply with the rigidity of separation between secondary and grammar schools in Northern Ireland's selective system. Secondly, overall attainment levels improved from 10% below the standard deviation of the national average in the 1977 cohort to 3% below in 1981 and then 13% above in 1985. These gains held across all social class levels when adjusted for the effects of socio-economic status. The authors conclude:

> For both sexes, the relationship between attainment and SES decreased across the three cohorts. The decrease was greater for males...This change indicates an increase in performance of low SES pupils relative to that of high SES pupils. (Wilms and McPherson; 1997. P.689)

The chief outcomes of comprehensive reorganisation in Scotland appear to have been social equalisation and academic improvement. In the first instance, inequality between pupils from different social class backgrounds was reduced relative to their experience of schooling, they met and worked with pupils from all backgrounds and abilities. This was achieved through the closure of small schools when selection at 12 was discontinued. The redefinition of catchment areas led to the educational and social benefits of able children with high expectations and a culture of learning studying alongside pupils from varying and often poorer social backgrounds.

Secondly, there has been a rise in average levels of attainment with the highest gains related to schools that had the longer experience of comprehensive education. The authors suggest that the schools 'learned how to improve'. They argue that:

> in a mere eight years, comprehensive reorganisation in Scotland significantly reduced social class inequalities of attainment that had been established over at least six decades...What the quasi-experimental design (of the research) fails above all to capture is the sheer historical accumulation of interest and power that confronted the school reforms of the 1960s and 1970s. (Ibid; P.689)

Their last conclusion could be a fitting description of the problem facing those who wish to reform secondary schooling in Northern Ireland. Central to the difficulties of removing selection is the perception of grammar schools as a 'gold standard' in the same way as A levels are regarded as the academic benchmark for the 16-19 year old age group despite attempts by the Dearing Inquiry into post-16 qualifications to introduce an 'applied' A level. Employers, it appears, remain familiar with and appreciate the qualities that a person with three good A levels brings to their business.

In addition, Northern Ireland's geographical position on the edge of the United Kingdom is matched by its economic marginality: there have always been higher levels of unemployment, greater poverty and lower expectations of health than in other parts of the United Kingdom. Against these bleaker aspects of Northern Irish life, education in general, has for most people shone out as one of the province's success stories, its 'gold standard'. For many, the argument is supported by the perceived excellence of schools, their good discipline record and especially the above average A level results achieved by the grammar schools where 70% leave with at least two A levels. The retention of traditional approaches or what was referred to earlier as the best aspects of the 'elementary tradition' in primary schools, held in high esteem by parents, is often quoted as the basis of pupils' later success. The fact that more children leave with poor and, in employment terms, unmarketable qualifications is somehow seen as an unfortunate by-product in people's perceptions and defence of the selective system. With 32% of pupils who took GCSE leaving with D-G grades in addition to 7% of boys and 3.5% of girls without any passes, it remains a serious and entrenched problem of the system.

This pattern of under-achievement is often popularly regarded as a temporary blemish on an otherwise high quality system or, more cynically, that too many of the secondary schools are failing. Under-achievement remains insufficiently connected with the consequences of telling the majority of pupils that they have 'failed' at the first major educational hurdle of selection. The problem is, in a sense passed on to the secondary schools, many of which face the task, often successfully, of re-building their pupils' confidence and to re-capture them academically. Explanations of the problem also ignore the debilitating impact on the morale and academic culture of secondary schools as a result of the grammar schools' increasing academic creaming of the 11 year old age group by digging deeper into the ability range than their original 'mission' intended. Gallagher in his evidence to the Northern Ireland Select Committee in 1996 showed that, despite the depredations of some of the grammar schools a number of secondaries succeeded in sending their pupils to higher education, including 26 where a tenth of pupils gained entry to a university. However, in 37 secondary schools 50% and more left without any GCSEs at grade C or above.

DENI has been successful in reducing the numbers leaving with poor results, not least because the 1989 reforms now require pupils to sit a terminal examination, although this trend had been obvious since the middle 1970s as credentialism became more apparent through increases in employers' expectations of young people's skills and knowledge. The latest school-focused programme is the Raising Schools' Standards Initiative targeting secondary and primary schools in areas with deeply entrenched patterns of economic and social disadvantage and low attainment levels. Eligibility for free school meals has been one of the main identifiers (although there is some dispute about this, (see McGill's; 1996b, evidence to the Northern Ireland Select Committee) and the schools have had to aim towards agreed attainment targets supported by frequent inspections to encourage and assess progress. It is about to be developed further by the recently announced (February 1998) School Improvement Project.

There is, however, another aspect to the problem of low attainment involving employers who, although they might publicly say that they need a more highly skilled workforce, nevertheless offer work at the lowest common denominator of skills and knowledge. In a survey of firms on the Isle of Sheppey, for example, Pahl (1985) found that for 85% of workers their most complicated daily task was driving to work. The low level of skills and qualifications among British 16 year olds may be a reflection of their view that there is no real incentive to invest in study in order to acquire better results. This may be related to companies' low demands because of the chronic short-termism of financial markets and investment. Finegold (1993) argues that the United Kingdom is caught in a 'low-skill equilibrium': bluntly speaking that employers get no more in skills than is warranted given the nature and quality of the work and the products that are turned out:

> Applying this framework to the British case it becomes apparent that the economy has been trapped in a low-skill equilibrium in which the majority of enterprises staffed by poorly trained managers and workers produce low quality goods and services… it will not pay individuals to remain in education to develop technical skills if companies are not prepared to invest in the research and development, new technologies and training required to make a high-skill strategy work. Likewise, managers will be reluctant to reorganise the work process and make these new investments if they do not have access to a supply of well-educated workers and new recruits. (P.69)

Selection and Identity

Questions of political and cultural identity explain why, to a significant extent Northern Ireland, contrary to the rest of the United Kingdom, has retained a system-wide selection process for children of eleven despite the substantial criticism that the procedure has received as well as its technical inaccuracies. In the first instance, the emergence of a self-aware and confident Catholic middle class has been attributed to the way in which grammar schools acted, in the eyes of successful Catholics, as 'engines' of social mobility for their children during the 1950s, 60s and 70s. This occurred in the face of direct discrimination in employment and more obliquely by the suppression of Nationalist or Irish cultural symbols and references in official representations of Northern Ireland. It remains the case, however, that the greater number of those leaving with poor qualifications come from Catholic secondary schools, 26% as compared to 23% in the state and other voluntary sectors. These figures, however, need to be interpreted against the background of the greater extent of social and economic disadvantage in the Catholic community because of the history and effects of discrimination. Taking entitlement to free meals as an indicator, Catholic secondary schools are the worst-off sector averaging 46% of pupils in this category. At the opposite end there were only 3% of pupils in Protestant grammar schools where the overall grammar school sector entitlement is on average 9% (McGill; 1996b).

In addition, the 1991 SACHR report (Cormack et al; 1991) found evidence that the Catholic sector as a whole had been under-funded for most of the period since partition. Whilst there was no evidence that this was caused by direct discrimination, the report argued that it was nevertheless bound to affect the facilities and by extension the performance of the schools. The differential arose mostly from the pattern of funding which tended to favour schools with larger grounds and more teaching space, categories where Protestant schools predominate. Estimates suggested that the funding gap over the period could be as much as £20m and that it is a significant factor in explaining the attainment gap at the upper and lower ends of examination achievement between Catholic and Protestant pupils.

Protestants share with Catholics a pride in their schools and the underlying message that education is something in which they excel despite other economic and political disadvantages. Politically, the success of Protestant grammar school pupils in achieving higher A levels passes than their counterparts in similar schools in Great Britain is perceived as an important part of Protestants' sense of self and community worth. Expressed loosely as a collective consciousness, it is allied to a feeling of themselves as an industrious people wedded to the ideal of self-help as a means of succeeding. Education is for many, central to this view of Protestant culture and, in the past, this was largely interpreted as British in orientation to the extent that Irish history, for example, was largely omitted from the curriculum of state secondary and Protestant grammar schools. This has been rectified so that both sets of pupils follow the same programmes in history, including Irish sections, as well as all other subjects of the now statutory curriculum. Both communities' interests in retaining 'their' grammar schools are represented by the Governing Bodies Association. The Association represents the views of the voluntary Catholic and Protestant grammar schools in any policy discussions with the government and has, as a result, a formidable degree of cross-community political legitimacy apart from any educational arguments that it might put forward for the retention of selection. Its member schools, whilst remaining separate and independent, have been vigilant in their scrutiny of government policy with regard to any perceived weakening of the DENI's commitment to the grammar school sector. They were successful in 1989, for instance, in rejecting government policy of bringing them under local authority control. With such a degree of cross-denominational consensus, it would be a rash government minister who attempted overtly to abandon selection in its present form.

Selection as a 'high stakes' test and its crucial significance for pupils' future education and prospects in life is, however, a throwback to a society where birth, social class and gender determined one's progress in life. It frustrates the pursuit of equality through educational opportunity which was the original aim of the introduction of secondary education for all children in 1944 and 1947 in Northern Ireland. The evidence indicates that it does this by sustaining the underlying persistence of social class as a determinant of success in the 11+ and especially so in the case of those from disadvantaged backgrounds. The recent figures from the DENI showing a strong negative link between entitlement to free school meals and success in the 11+ under-scores this point strongly. Their figures show:

> a strong association over time between social deprivation and the performance of pupils in the Transfer Procedure test, with pupils in higher free school meal schools doing less well. This association has become more pronounced for some groups notably those at either end of the deprivation scale, since 1993-94 when the Transfer Tests were changed from a verbal reasoning format to a curriculum orientated format. In 1995-96 pupils in those schools with the lowest proportion of pupils entitled to free school meals (FSM) were more than three

times as likely to achieve a grade A as those in the highest FSM schools. A substantially larger proportion of Catholic pupils attend schools in the high FSM categories. (DENI; 1996. P.1-2)

Originally, intelligence testing was meant to be a scientifically sound way out of the limitations of disadvantage, social position, race and gender based mostly on the work of Sir Cyril Burt the most eminent psychologist of the 1930s, 40s and 50s. From the work of Kamin (1974) and Schiff and Lewontin (1986), however, it is clear that much of the original statistical and theoretical basis for testing at 11 carried out in the 1930s by Burt is deeply flawed.

Such ascribed qualities, inherited from birth and wealth, were meant to be rendered obsolete through equality of access to education by matching natural ability with educational opportunity. In this way a child's educational outcomes and future lifechances were to be determined not by the circumstances of birth or class background but by achievement. Natural talent was to be freed, as far as possible, from the inequalities that such ascriptive qualities in the past imposed upon an individual's progress in life. Such equalising policies inevitably came up against the practical problems posed by the competition for resources as democratic governments attempted to meet their commitments in health, defence, foreign affairs and so on. Testing was originally introduced as a fair means of allocating finite resources in so far as it matched ability with, at the time in the United Kingdom, three different educational pathways. The justification for selection to these pathways, and the differentials of rewards they entailed, was that it contributed to the common good at a practical level by distributing scarce resources on the basis of natural talent rather than ability conferred by the advantages of social and economic privilege. It became clear by the late 1950s that social origins continued to exert a strong influence on the outcome of selection when Douglas found that the proportions of working and middle class children gaining access to grammar schools were similar to those before the introduction of the tri-partite system in 1944 (Douglas; 1964).

Recent findings in Northern Ireland by Northern Ireland Council for Educational Research (Wilson; 1985) and the Equal Opportunities Commission for Northern Ireland (Gallagher et al;1995) reflect a similar pattern. The different qualifications obtained by grammar and secondary pupils continued to lead to social and economic inequalities. These were determined mostly by the differentially rewarded occupational ladders that their educational qualifications entitled them to enter. Modern governments have tended to legitimise this on the grounds that unequal rewards are essential for attracting suitable candidates for functionally central jobs crucial to the well being of society and, by extension, for the common good of all. The legitimacy of such a position depends on the government's guarantee that the selective procedure is fair. More generally, at the level of giving justification for a range of public policies, that wealth and social position are attained and rewarded justly according to merit and not on the basis of ascriptive inequalities arising from birth, gender and class and in Northern Ireland religion. Bell (1972) gives a clear definition of this approach:

> The post-industrial society, in its logic, is a meritocracy. Differential status and differential income are based on technical skills and higher education, and few high places are open to those without such qualifications. (P. 30)

The underlying political and moral position of modern democratic but, it is argued, necessarily hierarchical societies is that the superior rewards enjoyed by the social and economic elites arising from the different types of education are perceived to be deserved. The democratic safety valve is that selection remains based on merit. If this ceases to be the case then, not only is equality of education inaccessible, but 'rule by the cleverest people' and the high salaries and social positions they enjoy are discredited. If, in other words, natural talent is not being used to its fullest and most equitable extent then access to positions central to the proper running of society is more apparent than real. The essentially meritocratic basis of modern societies is undermined if the older ascriptive qualities of social class origins continue to impose a defining influence on educational selection and outcomes. Education, in its role as the prime system for identifying talent in order that it is harnessed for the general good, becomes distorted if, in the case of Northern Ireland grammar schools, pupils continue to be drawn disproportionately from non-manual backgrounds and working class pupils pre-dominate in secondary schools. Research by the NICER (1985) shows that a child from a non-manual working background is 2.6 times more likely to gain access to a grammar school than a working class child. In terms of achievement the Northern Ireland Economic Council argues that the gap in attainment between grammar and secondary school leavers:

> ...may occur as a result of the demotivation of students who are assessed as academically less able and because more able students, whose presence may help to raise the attainment of less able groups, are educated separately. Recent research on the Northern Ireland educational system raises real doubts about whether it is possible to raise the standards of secondary students substantially within the present system of selection at the age of eleven. (NIEC; 1995. P. 73)

The original premises of testing at eleven and selection for different types of school seem increasingly to belong to another more ascriptive era. These are be summed up by Fraser (1997) as:

> intelligence can be described as a single score; that it is capable of ranking people in some linear order; that it is genetically based; and that it is immutable...it ignores the past 100 years of biological, psychological and anthropological research that challenges the notion of a single, uniform, and innate human intelligence, or *g*...(There are) multiple intelligences; practical, social, musical, spatial...(P.781)

The practical effect of selection can be seen from the numbers of pupils in the secondary sector who at the first opportunity 'vote with their feet' and leave for work or training scheme. The evidence internationally is that school leavers in the United Kingdom as a whole are under-qualified and particularly so in Northern Ireland. For those leaving with the equivalent of one GCSE at A to C in 1990-91 the relative figures are:

Table 4.1   Academic Qualifications: International Comparisons

Germany	62%
France	66%
Japan	50%
England	27%
Northern Ireland	22%

Source: NIEC (1995; P.35) and the Northern Ireland Council for Schools Examinations and Assessment.

At the other end of the school leavers' qualifications scale, the high attainment levels of A level students in Northern Ireland compared with the aggregated figures above, would indicate that the system works well for children who come from an affluent background, but that it under-achieves for the broad mass of pupils in comparison to other developed nations. Such a pattern is in large part caused by the historical emphasis in British education on academic qualifications most recently demonstrated in the argument surrounding the protection of A levels as the academic 'gold standard' and the seeming impossibility of its reform in any meaningfully vocational way, at least in the eyes of politicians, students and parents. The impact of this elitist intellectual tradition has been effectively to diminish the value and academic currency of parallel vocational education. Again recent research by the National Foundation for Educational Research (NFER) in relation to choice and participation rates in GNVQs and A levels, shows that in a sample of 435 schools offering these qualifications, 42% of students at foundation and intermediate GNVQ levels withdrew because of poor motivation or they took up jobs during the course (Sharp and Kendall; 1996). In contrast, only 9% of A level students left before completion. However, other research in Scotland suggests that the boundary between the two types of course is weakening although the vocational remains secondary to the Scottish Highers, the equivalent to A levels:

> Although the (Scottish) National (vocational) Certificate may be weakening the boundaries between academic and vocational courses in general secondary schools there are problems, in particular their secondary role and status and the haphazard nature of some modular (vocational) provision in some schools...Their role is still secondary to that of the Scottish Certificate of Education provision and to Highers in particular. (Howieson; 1993. P. 177-187)

Conclusion

Selection was originally introduced as a means of opening up access to forms of education that had been available only to a privileged minority or through a limited number of scholarships for very able pupils from mainly working class backgrounds. The provision of an open form of secondary education combining academic and vocational pathways was part of a more general change in the movement from an ascriptive society in which social position, education and employment were relatively fixed by factors such as gender, social origins, race and religion. The change involved a society where achievement depended on a person realising their natural talent through schooling and work, or more generally, that merit replaced privilege as the guiding principle for the allocation of pupils to school and work. The democratising role of education was central in providing the new social attitudes and political principles, in the widest sense, that would enable people to take a full and critical part in a more inter-dependent and competitive society. By the 1950s, however, the original principle of parity of esteem for the three forms of secondary schooling had been largely eroded by the primacy in the eyes of parents and employers of the grammar schools. This preference reflected a number of assumptions about and experiences of education, the most important of which was the added value that grammar schools delivered in their pupils' better access to higher education, the professions and other secure and well paid occupations compared to secondary modern schools. It had also become clear by then that the founding principle of matching natural talent with achievement outcomes, by removing the impediments of social origins, had been frustrated to a significant extent by the disproportionate presence of middle class children in the grammar schools relative to their numbers in the wider society. The selection test as the main instrument of selection for the different pathways became increasingly suspect because of the difficulty of devising any test of intelligence that was culturally or socially unbiased. The basic tenets of psychometric testing, that intelligence was innate, largely inherited, a unitary attribute and that it was fixed at birth also came under greater criticism to the extent that, combined with its social inequity, it was abandoned in the state sector schools in England and Wales during the 1960s and in Scotland during the early 1970s.

In the retention of selection, Northern Ireland appears to be caught in a time warp in regard to the continued inequity of the outcomes of selection in its bias towards children from affluent backgrounds. Education policy across the whole system has been affected in some way through the lens of selection and the need to protect the province's grammar school 'gold standard'. Even the introduction of a common curriculum providing identical coverage of subject content in the two types of school has left selection unaffected other than its adaptation of that curriculum as the means of selection at 11+. This is the more remarkable in the light of selection being at first premised on the theory that the post-11 curriculum should be anything but common: that one should be chiefly based on abstract and theoretical learning and the other practical and vocationally oriented.

The present form of testing has, moreover, become detached from the general movement towards criterion based assessment offering more valid measurements of individual potential against competency standards agreed by skilled practitioners. In contrast, the present selection test measures a pupil's ability against a norm or standard determined, in this case, by a combination of the places available in the grammar schools and an assumption, based on research now regarded as highly suspect, about the proportions of children thought capable of coping and benefiting from the different types of curriculum offered by the two sorts of school. As a 'high stakes' test it has important consequences for pupils' placement given the added educational value of grammar schools in attainment and future employment prospects. In this context, its predictive value gives cause for concern since about one in six pupils are wrongly placed. In addition, a number of secondary pupils transfer into grammar school after the review procedure at the end of second year and also at sixth form level with good GCSE results: pupils who had initially been thought unsuitable for this type of provision.

In terms of preparing pupils for work, selection in its present form belongs to a period when work skills for the greater proportion of manual workers were largely divorced from schooling: apprentices learned what they needed to know on the job from a 'journeyman'. Until 1944/47 the public elementary schools provided basic levels of literacy and numeracy for the majority of pupils, destined for this type of work. The secondary intermediates (secondary moderns in Great Britain) were meant to give this tradition a new and improved status by calling it vocational education where, it was initially thought, pupils would be free from the pressure of taking public examinations in order that they could concentrate on the skills needed for the mainly craft or semi-skilled work in which it was thought secondary pupils would be largely employed. It was only through the reforms of the late 80s, which compelled all pupils to take a public examination at the end of their time in school, that parents and the government were able to measure the successes and shortcomings of the whole sector. The numbers sitting examinations has been steadily increasing from the 60s onward as credentialism gained momentum and as the nature of work changed requiring higher levels of literacy and numeracy. The grammar schools' largely academic curriculum and the secondary sectors' vocational syllabuses reflected a wider division of labour based on the distinction between knowledge as concept and knowledge as execution. The former, it was thought, provided the basis for the professions and other high status work restricted to a minority of people who, it was assumed by the framers of the 1944 Act, needed to be selected early in order that they might attain the fullest understanding and depth of knowledge required for these positions. It was assumed that specialising in particular forms of subject based knowledge which made up the academic curriculum in the grammar schools was the best preparation for such central key positions, the more esoteric it became the greater prestige it attracted.

Changes in the nature of employment since the 1940s and 50s from a predominantly manufacturing base to a service oriented economy have eroded this distinction with the emphasis now on cerebral skills rather than basic manual strength or routine secretarial work. The taken-for-granted gender distinction in such a division of labour is another aspect of work that has altered radically since then. The globalisation of economies has meant increasing competition among nation states to attract multi-national firms to

95

their economies by offering tax incentives and, increasingly, skilled and well-educated work forces. The dramatic changes in communication and production technology, for example, have placed a premium on a country's workforce to be competent in the use of these technologies and to have sufficiently flexible knowledge skills to adapt to the inevitable changes in the technologies. Just as the former definitions of work as either mental or physical labour are becoming redundant it seems also that the distinction between academic and vocational knowledge is coming under scrutiny. The original differentials of knowledge and skills, which provided the rationale for early selection of pupils and also matched in the past by similar hierarchies of curriculum and employment, seem now to be increasingly arcane.

The current system of selection also raises wider policy questions of social justice in the extent to which it is socially divisive. The grammar-secondary differentiation is, in other words, a synonym for wider socio-economic distinctions of wealth, opportunity and prestige by the fact of the grammar schools' predominantly middle class enrolments and the secondary sector's chiefly working class composition. From this pattern of enrolments, the secondary schools suffer three disadvantages:

- the de-motivating effects of pupils' experience of early 'failure';

- the concentration of social and economic disadvantage in the sector as represented by an unequal proportion of their pupils compared to the grammar schools; and

- the academically debilitating effects of the grammar schools accepting a wider range of ability than was originally intended.

The loss of pupils in and around the selection borderline has been to the detriment of the whole learning culture of the secondary schools by reducing further pupils' range of intellectual experience than they would otherwise obtain in a school with an all-ability intake. One of the most signal research findings in Rutter et al's (1979) '15,000 Hours', which stimulated much subsequent work on school improvement, was the need for the full spread of ability in a school's intake if it was to develop a successful 'culture of learning'. The current pattern of a socially skewed recruitment to the two sectors undermines the more general meritocratic basis of modern democracies by the persistence, through selection at 11, of social origins in determining schooling and later employment and lifechances. The guiding principle of post-primary education is that it should be freely provided by the government to all according to age and aptitude and, in the original framers' minds, that social origins should no longer be the determining influence in a child's experience of schooling. Selection in its present form appears to run counter to this basic democratic premise.

Policy options in Northern Ireland with respect to selection seem constrained by the popularity of the grammar schools in securing access to higher education and better paid, higher status work. Parents know that a place at a grammar school means that their children enter a high expectation and achievement culture created by the school and pupils alike. In addition, they are largely free of serious discipline problems as are most of the secondary intermediates. Another factor is the way in which the sector is locked into the two communities' wider perceptions of what they value in their respective cultures. For Catholics, grammar schools remain a way out of the after-effects of employment discrimination where their children continue to suffer higher levels of unemployment than their Protestant counterparts. For Protestants, the schools appear to be an important component of their self-worth as a community. The schools' success is seen as one way of preventing the continual potential for marginalisation implicit in their political and geographical situation on the periphery of Europe. Both communities take pride in the fact that because of the quality of the grammar schools their children can compete with pupils from anywhere in the United Kingdom. These positive views of the selective system obscure underlying and strategically important difficulties identified by the Standing Commission for Human Rights:

> the elitism inherent in Northern Ireland's educational system is ultimately self-defeating. Hence, a starting point for reducing Northern Ireland's high unemployment levels lies in a reform of its education and training structure. (McGill; 1997. P.38)

Selection gives the grammar sector a clear intellectual rationale in the pursuit, essentially, of A levels and higher education places for its pupils. Whilst academic excellence is a proper aspiration for all children, it has come to dominate the whole system to the extent that the secondary schools, in order to sustain their enrolments, have felt the need to compete with the grammar schools. The idea of vocational education and the sorts of qualifications offered, such as NVQs and GNVQs are struggling to establish their validity and reliability in the eyes of pupils, grammar schools in particular and employers. Such attitudes stem from a deeper historical divide at the heart of British intellectual culture reflecting a society where only a small elite needed to acquire the high levels of knowledge needed to understand the basis of power and the best means of preserving and exercising it.

In the past, what became known as the academic curriculum; that is syllabuses that were highly abstract, past-oriented, strongly literal and divorced from everyday practical knowledge were the main gateway to university and the elite professions and other influential occupations close to power. In the nineteenth and a large part of the twentieth centuries social class, gender, and in Northern Ireland religion, acted as the main method of selection for access to these posts as expressed through the schools that pupils attended. The elementary schools were intended to give an education that would equip the vast bulk of people for work in the factories and mills. It was accompanied by a strong current of social discipline reinforcing the wider patterns of social class, denominationalism in Ireland and gender differentials. Independent and especially the more exclusive public schools were the educational and social training grounds for those who would in future exercise power. Against this background, the 1944/47 Acts were truly ground-breaking intended, as they were, to open up formerly closed educational pathways and the jobs to which they led.

In Northern Ireland the question remains as to how far selection continues to frustrate the aims of achieving an equal and more vocationally open society. It would be naive, however, not to acknowledge the same question being asked in Great Britain where approximately 92% of pupils attend comprehensives in England and 98% in Wales and Scotland. Selection in various forms has made a comeback especially in relation to over-subscribed schools. The Prime Minister's recent political and moral difficulties in placing his son in a successful Roman Catholic grant maintained school rather than his local comprehensive is an indication of the quandary ambitious parents in England and Wales find themselves in if their preferred residential area is not matched by the quality of education offered by local schools. The existence of a small but highly influential independent/public school sector in England still represents some degree of academic creaming but comparisons between comprehensive and selective schools reveal that:

> The most reasonable conclusion (from research studies) is that any differences in the overall examination effectiveness of the two systems are small. However, once comprehensives have become established they appear to reduce social class differences in attainment. A return to selection on measured ability at eleven would initiate a further long period of instability and would probably reduce overall attainment. More significantly, all of the studies found that there were far larger differences between the examination success of different schools of the same type than between the average examination results of different systems, even after such factors as social class had been taken into account. (Walford; 1992. P.95)

Changes in policy affecting selection would, in the context of Northern Ireland, inevitably have to take account of Protestant and Catholic perceptions of 'their' grammar schools outlined earlier. On this basis, the view of the government is that there is no overwhelming desire among parents to abandon selection. Comprehensive schools will develop piecemeal, it is argued, driven in most instances by local circumstances. There are a small number of areas with pupils from one community or the other in the minority where an all ability comprehensive school has been created. Not least of the factors in this interplay of views and assumptions about the role of grammar schools are present levels of access put very conservatively at around 40% of the age group and in some areas considerably more. In favour of retaining selection, there is also the more relevant educational argument about matching the pace and depth of learning to pupils' natural ability in order that they realise their academic potential without undue delay. This is usually interpreted as the need to teach pupils with others of more or less the same ability which does not necessarily lead to the rigidities of streaming that has characterised British schools for most of the 20th century. Streaming was thought to be the most efficient way of teaching pupils given the limited resources available but it was also based on the mistaken view that intellectual ability was a unitary attribute and open to only minimal change. Other countries in Europe and elsewhere have developed more flexible arrangements for post-primary schooling involving delayed selection after which parents make the decision about the type of school their children will attend.

In France, for example, pupils transfer to a 'first cycle' college at age 12 during which pupils are taught a common curriculum with a minimum of differentiation. Ability is assessed according to their results and there is the possibility of being held back to repeat a year if these are poor. After completion of this phase at 15-16 years, parents in consultation with teachers can decide to take the longer course at the *lycée* leading to the *baccalaureat* including now a *baccalaureat de technicien*, or a variety of shorter courses leading to vocational certificates of differing levels of difficulty such as the three year *brevet de technicien* or the two year *brevet d'études professionel*. These are now taken at the up-rated *lycées d'enseignment profesionel* in order to give them the same public status as the traditional highly esteemed academic *lycées*. These arrangements have produced a number of enviable outcomes: a participation rate of 92% for 16 year olds compared with 75% in the United Kingdom. Higher rates of staying-on apply also at 17 and 18 with the result that 66% of pupils in this age group achieved the equivalent of a CCSE pass at A-C in mathematics, French, and one science in contrast to

27% in England and Wales and 22% in Northern Ireland. This pattern is repeated in most of mainland Europe. There is a difficulty in making such direct comparisons because of our different philosophical and educational histories. The intellectually Olympian *Grand Ecoles* represent the zenith of higher education in France and have, since their inception over 200 years ago, combined professional, academic and technical knowledge in their curricula. The *Grand Ecole Polytechnique*, for instance, would provide engineers with the relevant science, a full professional training combined with general education directly applied to their career. The distinction between academic and vocational education has been less evident and as a result technical training courses have greater currency and prestige among parents and employers than their counterparts in the united Kingdom.

In Northern Ireland, the two-tier, junior/senior high school arrangements in the Craigavon area provide a starting point for reviewing the current pattern of post-primary schooling. Whilst it has several problems not least of which is the proximity of grammar schools where some parents from the two-tier system area prefer to send theirchildren thus depriving the Craigavon schools of the full range of ability. The evidence quoted earlier indicates that, in terms of predicting future attainment, selection at the end of the junior cycle was a better predictor than at the earlier age of 11. In addition, pupils selected at age 14 who went on to the academically oriented senior high schools achieved, on average, better results than pupils who started in grammar schools at age 11 (Wilson and Gardiner; 1982). In terms of equity the two-tier system appears to provide a more measured opportunity to assess a pupil's progress and for making crucially important decisions about his or her future educational pathway that will in turn affect employment and more generally the quality of their lifechances. Without reform the system will go further down the road in the:

> …development of a hierarchy of schools which will provide the poorest education for those children most in need and the best for those who already have the most advantages. (Walford; 1992. P.90)

Disadvantage and Educational Intervention Policy

From the figures used in the discussion on Northern Ireland's selective system there is clearly a problem of under-achieving pupils and schools. It has also been argued that this is not solely a Northern Ireland problem: in international comparisons pupils from the United Kingdom as a whole perform less well than pupils in comparable systems in Europe and elsewhere. In explaining the disparity, an initial problem lies in the ability of early leavers, at 15 and then after 1972 at 16, to opt out of taking a public examination leaving therefore with no public qualifications. The introduction of the Certificate of Secondary Education (CSE) as a lower tier alternative to GCE brought more pupils into the qualifications 'net'. Both examinations were replaced by GCSE in 1988 which meant that the greater majority would leave with a qualification that they could alternatively use as a foundation for further study or present to an employer or training agency. The introduction of examinations for all pupils reflects the changing pattern of employment as the need for manual and secretarial and other routine work requiring few qualifications and skills declined from the early 1970s onwards. Employers demanded greater levels of literacy and numeracy in their workforces although, as the earlier argument by Finegold showed, they often continued to organise work on a low-skill basis. Much of the clamour for more qualifications was fuelled by increasing credentialism. This has meant that, where formerly five GCEs secured entry to a number of occupations, a degree has now become the norm as the effects of a mass higher education system take hold with approximately 30% of 21 year olds holding degrees of some sort. There was also a more general educational argument that it was intrinsically worthwhile to educate children to their fullest possible potential and that examinations were one way of providing an incentive and also of measuring that achievement. It is arguable that schooling is now examination driven to an extent that their development never intended. The advent of greater accountability in education now means that pupils are tested at four Key Stages, at eight, (seven in England and Wales) 11, 14, and 16 on leaving school, the results of which are used to produce raw league tables of schools' performance.

The low level of some pupils' qualifications has concerned DENI, teachers, parents and employers since it was revealed in the 1980s that over 20% of pupils were leaving without any qualifications. The introduction of more public examinations, especially GCSE, has gone a long way towards reducing this proportion 4% in 1994-95 (DENI Statistical Release, December,1997). Higher ability pupils have also improved their performance with an increase of those with two or more A levels from 20% in 1985 to 31% in 1994-95. The range of grades in GCSE from A to G takes in a very wide range of ability and in relatively quick time the former GCEs re-asserted themselves as an academic standard for comparing the new GCSE grades. This has effectively diminished the value of grades D-G in the new examination by rendering, in the eyes of parents and employers, passes at A-C as equivalent to a pass at the former GCE level which they were familiar with and understood. An accepted benchmark for achievement is at least one GCSE at A-C as the objective for the minimum foundation level for the National Targets for Education and Training promoted by the Confederation of British Industry. The policy is meant to improve standards by aiming at targets for different stages in learning. For example, the Foundation Learning targets for young people up to age 21 are:

- at age 19 students should have NVQ level 2, an intermediate GNVQ, or five GCSEs at grade C or above;

- at 19 three-quarters of young people should have attained level 2 NVQ competence in communication, numeracy and information technology and 35% to achieve level 3 competence in these skills by age 21;

- by age 21, 60% of young people to achieve two A levels, an advanced GNVQ or NVQ level 3; and

- lifelong learning targets are also set for people in work.

Pupils obtaining passes at D-G and those leaving without any formal qualifications of any sort against these criteria can be defined as under-achieving. Taking these two categories together, there were about 37% of pupils in Northern Ireland in 1993-94 leaving with results about which employers will be sceptical as an indication of the young person's potential for making a good employee (McGill; 1982 and DENI Statistical Bulletin; 1997).

Applying the ideas surrounding the current discussion about added value when interpreting examination performance, the results above need to be related to the circumstances of the schools and areas in which pupils live; their socio-economic backgrounds the social and academic mix in the school. Combining GCSE results with socio-economic indicators, the three highest scores were obtained by pupils who were ineligible for school meals, had both parents working and attended grammar school. The three lowest scores are a reverse image of these and concerned pupils who were at secondary school, had both parents unemployed and were eligible for free school meals. (Gallagher et al; 1997, P.66). The effects of social disadvantage are apparent in these figures with the greater impact experienced by Catholic pupils where the academic indicator was lower than for Protestant pupils. This pattern reflects the higher levels of socio-economic deprivation among Catholic communities than Protestants in terms of their relative incomes.

Table 4.2   Religious Affiliation and Income

Religion	All	Cath.	Prot.	None
Gross household income	%	%	%	%
Less than £8000 p.a.	50	59	47	42
£18,000 or more	18	15	21	20

Source: British Social Attitudes; Jowell 1990

The figures above need to be qualified in the light of the average size of family in the two communities: Catholic families have on average 3.6 persons compared with 2.7 for Protestants experiencing, therefore, a greater degree of relative poverty than Protestant families because of the need to spread the family's income more thinly. If retired persons are omitted from these figures (there are a greater number of retired Protestants) the gap becomes much wider: approximately two in five Protestant families had incomes of less than £8 ,000 compared with over half of Catholic families. Conversely, about a quarter of Protestant households had incomes over £18,000 whereas only one in six Catholic families had a similar income. More general indices of imbalances between the two communities can be observed in terms of social class and their respective experiences of unemployment. Forty-seven% of Catholics compared with 33% of Protestants were in working class occupations and one in six economically active Catholics were registered unemployed; the comparable figure for Protestants was one in ten.

The impact of differential experience of disadvantage on educational achievement can be gauged from the entrenched attainment gap between Catholic and Protestant pupils which has been sustained despite the overall improvement in pupils' results. In Catholic managed schools there has been an enhancement of performance of 10% in pupils attaining five or more GCSEs or NVQ equivalents from 38% in 1989-90 to 48% in 1994-95. In the predominantly Protestant schools the improvement was 17.3% a rise from 38.3% to 55.6% over the same period (DENI). The gap in results has improved from 3.9% to 3.6%, but it persists and is a barrier to creating equity of employment opportunity. The importance of this gap can be seen by the relationship between qualifications and employment: in Northern Ireland people without any qualifications are twice as likely to be unemployed as those with GCSEs or the former GCEs and ten times more likely than graduates who will also on average earn ten times more.

Raising School Standards Initiative

In attempting to improve the attainment of under-achieving, poorly qualified for work pupils from disadvantaged areas, the government introduced the Raising School Standards Initiative (RSSI) in 1995-98 designed to concentrate on and raise the academic performance of primary and post-primary schools in disadvantaged areas. It is part of a wider policy of targeting social needs (TSN) in order that money designated for alleviating poverty and educational disadvantage is concentrated on those who need it most and where it can do most good. Such a policy will succeed best when the correct criteria for distribution are drawn up and this has caused some disagreement and produced anomalies in relation to the inclusion of some schools and the exclusion of others. McGill in his evidence to the Northern Ireland Select Committee in 1996 shows some significant variations in the amount that schools received from TSN funds and, in a related way, whether they were included or excluded in the initiative according to the different criteria used.

In allocating TNS funds, the Belfast Board, for instance, applies a threshold of 20% of pupils eligible for free school meals before a school receives anything, whereas other Boards allocate on an individual basis. These results in Belfast awarding a higher amount than the other Boards: £360 per pupil as opposed to £275 in the Western Board and £220 and £235 in others. Another anomaly, he claims, is the higher amounts allocated directly by the DENI to voluntary grammar and integrated schools £285 and £253 respectively and the fact that some grammar schools with FSM rates as low as 0.3% receive TSN funds. The seven different formulae used by the different bodies responsible for distribution of the funds led to one school with 36 FSM pupils receiving £10,260 and another with the same number receiving nothing. Another state funded grammar school having 93 FSM pupils was allocated nothing whilst if it had have been a voluntary school it would have obtained £26,505 (McGill; 1996b). With regard to including schools in the RSSI programme, there appears to be some confusion and anomalies, McGill argues, arising from the criteria used by the DENI. These are a combination of examination results, truancy rates and FSM entitlement as opposed to the single FSM index in more common use by the Boards to distribute TSN money. The result of using only a combination of FSM and GCSE results as an index of disadvantage meant that the DENI was faced, with the fact that, since deprivation is significantly more prevalent in Catholic communities, the bulk of the funds should go to that sector rather than to Protestant areas. Catholic grammar schools, for instance, are six times more likely to have significant levels of disadvantage, (that is with more than 10% FSM pupils), than their Protestant counterparts. A similar pattern is evident in the secondary schools where only one Catholic School had less than 20% FSM pupils compared to twenty-five Protestant schools. The figures below express the overall pattern of free school meals entitlement.

Table 4.3   Free School Meal Entitlement by Sector and Religion, 1995-96

	<10%	10-20%	20-30%	30-40%	40-50%	>50%
Protestant grammar	38	2	0	0	0	0
Catholic grammar	6	15	10	0	0	0
All grammar	44	17	10	0	0	0
Protestant secondary	3	22	22	21	7	3
Catholic secondary	0	1	7	24	20	26
Integrated	0	1	1	3	0	0
All secondary	3	24	30	48	27	29

Source: McGill (1996b)

The imbalance is clear from these figures in the extent to which Catholic schools appear to be in greater need of RSSI funds. On the face of it, the larger portion of RSSI funds is needed in the Catholic schools if FSM entitlement is used as the main criterion. It has the merit of simplicity and acts as an accurate proxy for the circumstances of pupils from disadvantaged homes with regard to the amount of money coming into the family. The DENI's attempt to spread the funds more evenly by applying a wider spread of indicators of disadvantage was an attempt at drawing attention away from what would otherwise be criticised as a Nationalist bias. If, in other words, the money followed only the FSM index and the Department's addition of exam results the bulk of it would have gone to Catholic schools. In the event, pursuing a policy of what looks like equal shares towards the two sectors, rather than need, produced a number of oddities of inclusion and exclusion. Using only combined FSM and academic criteria to compare two Catholic secondary schools, for example, one with 62% of pupils entitled to free school meals and 48% attaining GCSE grades A-G was included in the initiative. Another, seemingly in more need of RSSI funds, having 66% FSM pupils and 38% at grades at A-G was excluded. This was in contrast to an included state school with 78% achieving GCSE at A-G, which is above the Northern Ireland secondary average, and 34% of FSM. These examples, and there are others, appear to be a result of the DENI attempting to ensure that some of the funds went to the state schools and thus avoiding any potential criticism of political imbalance (McGill; 1996b).

An added factor in a consideration of the government's policy towards improving the achievement of disadvantaged pupils is the extent to which selection appears to be 'a blow upon a bruise' with respect to the impact of poverty on pupils performance in the 11+.

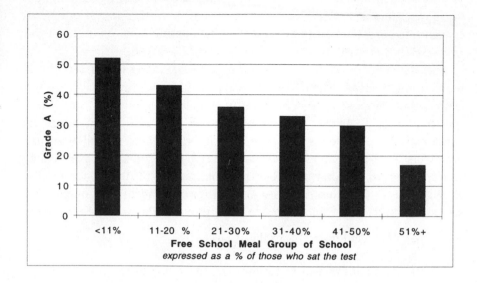

Figure 4.1   Grade 'A' by Free School Meal Group, 1995/96

Source: SB1/96, Department of Education for Northern Ireland

The evidence from the graph above suggests that affluence as a factor in obtaining an A grade has strengthened over the period from 1989-1996 judging from the DENI's statistics (DENI; 1996, SB1/96) and especially so since the change from a verbal reasoning test to an examination in maths, English and science. In 1995-96, 52% of pupils in the most prosperous schools obtained an A grade compared with 16% in the most disadvantaged schools. Because of the greater impact of disadvantage in Catholic schools, recent changes in the 11+ to an attainment test of curricular subjects have hit their pupils hardest and opened up a widening gap in passes between them and their Protestant counterparts. In 1995-96, figures from the DENI show that the percentage of Catholic pupils gaining the top A grades was seven points lower than those in the predominantly Protestant state schools. Before the changeover there had been relatively few differences, a finding consistent with the view that verbal reasoning tests in identifying intellectual ability are generally fairer to pupils from disadvantaged backgrounds. In 1991-92 pupils in Catholic schools having more than half FSM pupils achieved approximately 25% grade As; in 1993-94, following the change to an attainment test, the percentage went down to 20%. The rate has decreased further in the two succeeding years to 16% in

1995-96. In addition, the number of parents deciding not to enter their children for the test has increased from 30% to around a third, most of whom are concentrated in schools with high rates of FSM entitlement. Source; (DENI; 1996, SB1/96 Transfer Procedure Results 1989-90-95-96.)

In its Strategic Plan for Education 1996-2000, the DENI sets out its mission statement as: 'To provide the best possible opportunities for pupils to learn and develop, so as to help them fulfil their potential and contribute to society and the economy'. When reading this, it is difficult to escape the conclusion that, for every step forward the DENI makes in its policy towards improving schools, it is dragged two paces back by selection. This is especially so for pupils from poorer families whose ability to 'fulfil their potential' is already heavily circumscribed by unemployment and disadvantage. The argument could also be applied to the Department's other aims of promoting:

- self-esteem and respect for others; and

- an understanding and experience of the challenges and rewards of learning.

The document is, however, unequivocal in the retention of selection: 'The government's plans also reflect the following assumptions; that the selective system of secondary education will remain, though the Government is prepared to consider carefully any specific proposals for alternatives at local or regional level'. There is, however, a commitment in the Strategic Plan to RSSI through the allocation of additional funds to those schools that need it. In terms of how well the funds were targeted, however, the evidence from the Northern Ireland Select Committee in 1996, if correct, suggests that it is at best difficult to determine the true destination of the money and that needy pupils may not obtain the full intended advantage from RSSI funds. When the interviewee was asked by the chairman of the Select Committee about the different formulae used to allocate funds the reply was:

> First of all the five Education and Library Boards allocate money to secondary and maintained schools in their area and then the Department separately funds voluntary grammar schools. As each of these bodies has discretion to decide their own formula it means there are seven different ways of allocating money. ...Once the resources have been decided (by the Secretary of State) there are seven different formulae for allocating them to the schools.

More worrying still:

> One of the difficulties is that, although money is allocated on the basis of social deprivation, it is up to schools and Boards how they spend it. There is no

monitoring whatsoever. There are not even reports. I cannot go to any published document and find out how much was spent on social deprivation. It is not in their (schools) annual budget statements and it is not required to be, so I think there is a problem there. (McGill; 1996b)

The evidence seems to suggest that some schools receiving RSSI funds have interpreted this to mean that it is an addition to the overall budget rather than a 'ring-fenced' amount to be spent solely on ameliorating the circumstances of disadvantaged pupils and improving their academic performance. The DENI's difficulty in this is that such a prescriptive approach to the spending of RSSI funds would run counter to the principle and practice of their Local Management of Schools policy which gives Boards of Governors independence over about 85% of their budget.

The School Improvement Programme

The new programme to be introduced in September 1998 may have a more benign title than the more pointed RSSI which had a certain reformist ethos, but the new programme seems determined to continue the work and to apply any lessons learned from its predecessor. In a positive sense the DENI in its introduction to the programme states:

> Effective teaching is supported and made possible by effective school management. Where either is absent, the school will find it difficult to offer its pupils the quality of education which they deserve.

Taking this one stage further, the DENI reveals the harder edge of school improvement:

> It will therefore be important that ineffective teachers, principals or members of the senior management team are identified, so that Boards of Governors and Library boards and CCMS can offer them through the efficiency procedures ...support and opportunities to improve their performance...Where a satisfactory level of improvement does not prove possible within agreed timescales, however, Boards of Governors will be supported by Boards/CCMS in securing the discontinuation of the individuals's employment...(DENI; 1998. Para. 23-24)

For schools participating in the School Improvement Programme, there will be a period of three years in the first instance to turn themselves around as judged by inspections with a further two year extension. If the schools remain poor then mergers and closures will be considered. A school's performance will be considered against three criteria:

- quality of teaching;

- quality of school management and leadership; and

- school development plans, incorporating targets for improvement.

The programme is also firmly set within the context and outcomes of the RSSI although the latter is considered to be a success irrespective of any results that might come from an independent audit being conducted by the London Institute of Education. These are to be published early in 1999. From the DENI's documents it is somewhat unclear as to the role of the largely quantitative research undertaken by the Institute:

> During this final year, 1997-98, all participating schools will be visited by Inspectors to provide an evaluation of their current state of progress ...to confirm the Inspectorate's judgement of progress during the Initiative. In addition, a quantitative evaluation of RSSI, being carried out by The Institute of Education, University of London, *will contribute evidence of the impact of the initiative on pupils' performance in the participating schools.* (Para.10) (*Author's italics*)

Based on this statement it seems clear that the DENI's inspections will play the major part in reporting on the progress of RSSI and it also appears from the first sentence above that the inspectorate have already made up their minds about its success. This assertion, it is argued, is based on lessons learned from RSSI, chief of which is:

> ...as a strategy, school self-evaluation and a specific programme of self-improvement, supported by CASS (Curriculum Advisory and Support Service) works and, for most schools, works very successfully. (Para. 11)

Schools it is claimed:

> ...are developing a culture of continuous improvement, and a language in which to plan, to set targets and to address their key issues. (Ibid.)

Some qualification of this occurs in respect of RSSI schools which are persistently under-performing despite the support they have received from the initiative. With regard to these schools, the DENI appears to be resolute in dealing with them along the same lines as those in England and Wales by forming an 'action group' comprising the area Board or CCMS, local business interests or heads of other schools who have had similar problems and had dealt with them successfully.

Educational Disadvantage: Policy and Politics

The policy of improving under-achieving schools through the provision of a mixture of extra financial resources, curricular support and the threat of an 'action group' is part of a wider movement in government thinking as the New Right took increasing hold on educational policy during Mrs Thatcher's period as Prime Minister and continues to influence New Labour's mission to reform schools. This new thinking about education was born out of a disappointment with the post-war policies in education which were framed against the view that investment in the nation's human capital through a general increase in access to education at all levels would lead to greater prosperity. It was part of an underlying belief about what Goldthorpe (1968) has called 'the Logic of Industrialism'. This was a modernist view of the process of industrialisation; that it was an equalising process through the promotion of skill and industry's reliance on merit as a means of selecting people who would then work more efficiently, than former patterns of recruitment based on nepotism or class affiliation. Socially, it was based on a post-war consensus about the need for more education which would lead to the 'inefficient' aspects of our society such as the inequalities produced by social class differences eventually disappearing as people became more educated and able to compete on equal terms with others for society's 'goods'. Inequality, in this sense, was an aberration, a result of history and would become increasingly redundant.

The policy of equality of educational opportunity placed schools in a key position in creating a more equitable society. Schools would be able to select pupils on the grounds of their ability, initially identified by the 11+, and, on the basis of their progress at school, to allocate them fairly to the labour market. The policy was also framed against the view that the selection of pupils was just and that it was objectively determined. It was also a way of creating a common culture by promising all the differing communities, many of whom had been formerly excluded from a wide range of jobs and life experiences, that in future they could aspire to the highest occupations in terms of prestige and earnings. It was now the individual's responsibility to make maximum use of the educational resources available and that the impediments of social class as an explanation of low attainment and success would diminish to the extent of being no longer acceptable. The movement in educational thought was characterised by the replacement of individuals' ascribed qualities of birth, social class or gender, by their achievement within an educational system open to all according to merit. The introduction of comprehensive schools during the 1960s was the most recent phase of the realisation at an institutional level of such policies.

Current government policy on school improvement and pupils' under-achievement reflects a wider disappointment with this theory of education. It reflected the view among politicians and educationalists of the political right that schooling in this form had not led to prosperity and concurrently had played a large part in causing under-achievement. The cause lay in the autonomy given to the 'educational establishment' to develop what were criticised as unsuccessful progressive teaching methods, as opposed to 'tried and tested' more direct didactic approaches. Schooling had also become adrift from the needs of the economy, failing especially by turning out unproductive and under-skilled pupils many of whom were antipathetic towards work, a further consequence it was claimed of 'airy-fairy' notions of education. By this time the market had permeated nearly all aspects of government policy: in welfare benefits, health provision and latterly in education. Schools were allowed to opt out of local authority control and given the power to spend their budgets according to their own priorities through the policy of Local Management of Schools. The introduction of an educational market was part of a more general view that an important discipline for improving schools could be obtained from the needs of the economy: schools in future were to be tied more closely to the requirements of business. Vocational education was no longer to be the Cinderella of the curriculum whilst, contrariwise, A levels were retained as the academic 'gold standard' which was related to the New Right's wider claim of lower intellectual standards. The argument has meant the abandonment of the original aim of GCSEs as a common examination, as papers have become increasingly 'tiered' so that only able pupils are advised to enter for the higher level papers, with consequent intellectual devaluation of the others and the lower grades obtainable.

Post-war egalitarian policies towards schooling were also coming under criticism from more orthodox research on the extent to which opportunity was in practice open to all as measured by the outcomes. Jencks (1972) provided one of the most significant shocks to the consensus about the creation of equality through greater access to education, by showing that family background and other mainly class and ethnic factors were more important in determining a child's educational achievement and employment than schooling. On the political and educational left, Halsey and colleagues in 1980 published a comprehensive survey of the outcomes of post-war egalitarian British legislation in education and concluded that a middle-class boy was ten times more likely to be still at school at age 18 than his working-class counterpart and was eleven times as likely to go to university.

Later work by Halsey in 1993 suggests that more children from working class homes are going to universities in absolute terms but not in proportion to their overall numbers in the population. Pupils from affluent backgrounds were more than twice as likely to obtain a degree than if degree-holding were randomly distributed. Expressed as a ratio for entry to higher education it was 2.05 for pupils from affluent backgrounds compared 0.36 for children from semi-skilled and unskilled backgrounds. Pupils from skilled manual backgrounds had a ratio of 0.52. In similar vein, Bowles and Gintis (1976) writing about American education, argued that the chief role of schools was to instil respect for authority and the necessary disciplines in the future workforce. Schools, they argued, impose relationships that are scaled on a top-down basis, and teach obedience in direct reflection of the needs of industry. They also produce evidence that intelligence and attainment are relatively unimportant in attaining high earning jobs and that they act only as a screening device for employers. Whilst acknowledging the gains in literacy and personal fulfilment from education they nevertheless conclude that schools produce in many pupils a feeling of powerlessness often reproduced in their experience of work or unemployment, schools are:

> destined to legitimate inequality, limit personal development to forms compatible with submission to arbitrary authority, and aid in the process whereby youth are resigned to their fate. (P.266)

The French educationist, Pierre Bourdieu (1990) argues that schools are a means for the transfer of pupils' cultural capital into educational and occupational goods. This inevitably favours middle class children because of the structure and presentation of knowledge as well as the cultural and behaviour assumptions all of which are familiar to middle class children. Working class pupils, by contrast, he argues, find school to be an unfamiliar and alien environment leading to under-achievement and early leaving.

The process is well illustrated by Willis (1977) who shows how working class boys reproduce their cultural background by opting out of academic achievement and go on to jobs where they repeat their educational pattern of minimalism in their attitude to work. Their outwardly anti-school behaviour and lack of interest becomes, Willis suggest, a form of resistance to an alien culture:

> the 'lads' specialise in a caged resentment which always stops just short of outright confrontation. Settled in class, as near a group as they can manage, there is a continuous scraping of chairs, a bad-tempered 'tut-tutting' at the simplest request, and a continuous fidgeting about which explores every

permutation of sitting or lying on a chair…Opposition to the school is principally manifested in the struggle to win symbolic and physical space from the institution and its rules and to defeat its main perceived purpose: to make you 'work'. (PP. 12-13, 26)

The School Improvement Programme's support for under-achieving schools stems from a research tradition which, in testing these pessimistic views of the ability of universal education to promote greater equality of achievement, access to higher education and employment, found that schools do make a difference. Studies by Rutter (1979), Mortimore and colleagues (1988) and in Northern Ireland Caul (1994) and Daly (1991) indicate that, despite pupils' unpromising backgrounds, schools can make a significant impact, or what has become known as added value. This occurs outwardly where pupils make significantly more progress than could have been predicted from a consideration of their background and circumstances; especially so for disadvantaged children. Creemer (1994) argues that only 12 to 18% of differences in pupil attainment can be attributed to the effects of schooling compared to their backgrounds. Using value added scores, however, other research by Thomas and Mortimore (1994) suggests that a good school can make a difference for pupils in the likelihood of them achieving GCSE at grade C and, in a less successful one, the probability of an E grade.

The School Improvement Programme has included the harder New Right edge of exposing the schools that continue to fail to the market through mergers, dismissal of 'unproductive' management and classroom 'workers'. In addition, the fact of inclusion sends its own message to the market in terms of its effects on parents' perceptions of the schools and their attitude towards sending their children to them. At the other end of the achievement range, privilege has re-asserted itself as the criterion for educational and occupational success through middle class parents' ability to protect their increased access to grammar schools and the added value that they deliver. The social class bias evident in the selection test is the outward mechanism for this process, but the more general inflation of required qualifications for employment has also led to middle class pupils maintaining their academic advantage from the grammar schools and also in the job market. The evidence for this comes from the continuing growth of higher education, providing students with degrees for work where they formerly needed only O or A levels and, at the same time as Halsey shows, the persistent over-representation of students from affluent non-manual backgrounds at universities. In higher education, upper middle class students have protected their market position by their greater access to the 'old' pre-1992 universities and in terms of the implicit and explicit rankings of degrees employers make between the degrees offered by the 'old' and 'new' universities. Brown and colleagues (1997) argue that the expansion of higher education may be explained by the middle class's determination to protect their children's position in an increasingly insecure employment market demanding higher levels of qualification. Politically, all three main parties know that to impose any serious reduction of higher education would mean risking the loss of middle class votes.

The recent controversy over fees for students is an example of affluent families' hostile reaction to a policy with the potential for restricting access and diminishing their educational advantage and opportunity to acquire employment credentials at university. At the same time, however, such a policy secures their children's market position through their parents' greater ability to pay the costs of the fees. Since the removal of grants, the importance of middle class parents' ability to pay for their children's upkeep while they are at university will increase as the time needed to gain sufficient qualifications becomes longer in response to a credential-driven employment market. This is a form of economic screening for qualifications and the jobs they lead to by families needing to dig deeper into their resources in order that their children can invest more time in achieving the credentials necessary for selection for employment.

Taking the inspectorate's positive assessment of the RSSI at face value, a significant number of pupils have clearly benefited from the scheme although that assessment would be stronger if confirmed by the independent evaluation being conducted by the London Institute. In relation to the wider aspects of school improvement concepts, the programme has a number of significant limitations. The school improvement research shows clearly that, in the post-primary sector, schools achieve 'take-off' when a number of factors are put together. Sammoms et al, (1995) in summarising the findings of a large body of research list 11: the continued presence of selection appears to place limitations on several key elements. High expectations all round, for example, seems somewhat restricted when the ablest pupils are absent whilst paradoxically this aspect of the grammar sector is one the chief components of the added value that the schools deliver. This criticism applies also to the need for intellectual challenge and the fact that the pupils who could provide the stimulation at the top end of that challenge are in another sector running in parallel but, as in geometry, never meeting.

Equality of opportunity policies in the period since 1944, in turning away from selection at 11, were founded on the principle that it was a self-evident human right of children to study and mix with pupils of all abilities. The creaming effect of selection denies disadvantaged children this central democratising opportunity. Another central feature of improving school standards concerns raising pupil esteem, especially important in the context of the multiple disadvantages that many of the pupils in the programme schools suffer. For many secondary schools, this presents an added disadvantage in their task of stimulating their pupils to work for educational achievement. More generally, there remains the question of the central purpose of the secondary schools. Are they to be 11-16 schools preparing pupils for entry to the 11-18 grammar schools or should they be allowed to develop in the fullest sense their own intellectual and vocational integrity rather than as preparation grounds for grammar school sixth forms? If it is the former, then selection no longer has any purpose if pupils are to be encouraged to stay on at school after the age or 16. This will become more important as vocational qualifications gradually achieve parity with A levels. If the secondary schools are to achieve academic integrity in its full sense of 11-18 schools, then selection seems equally redundant.

5 The Policy Process: Interviews with Policy Makers

Influence and Power in Framing and Implementing Education Policy

In earlier chapters it was argued that Northern Ireland's education system is similar to most other parts of the United Kingdom in its management by local Education and Library Boards and central government in the form of the DENI. It differs significantly, however, in the extent to which the voluntary principle plays a central role in the framing of policy. The principle is represented directly first by the Catholic Church as owners of the maintained primary and secondary schools and indirectly by the Protestant Churches in the state schools through their rights as transferors. The second group comprises the Catholic and Protestant voluntary grammar schools which make up the bulk of the province's selective sector and have played a pivotal role in the retention of selection at 11 for approximately 90% of pupils. Beyond these outwardly visible policy making and influence groups there is also a complex network of local and Westminster politicians and community groups and other professional bodies such as the teacher unions which all, to a greater or lesser extent, bring some degree of influence to bear. The interviews set out here show the way in which some of the key groups and individuals interpret and influence the policy process and its outcomes. The interviews were semi-structured and include indepth discussion of:

- the location and use of power within the system in implementing policy;

- the application of the principle of equity as it is realised through the system of schooling in Northern Ireland; and

- questions surrounding perceptions of the legitimacy of the way in which policy is currently framed.

The first group of interviews involve three Chief Executive Officers (CEO) of the Education and Library Boards. The first was with the recently retired Chief Executive of the Board covering part of Belfast and the more rural region to the south and east. He had substantial first hand experience of the system having spent 18 years teaching in primary, post primary schools and in a college of education, all within the Catholic sector. At the time of the interview he had been in post for eight years. The second is currently in post with responsibility for the Belfast area and who originally came from industry and further education. The third also recently retired, came through the controlled school system. In discussing relationships with the DENI there was an impression that, although these were generally good, there was nevertheless little leeway if the Department decided on a particular course of action:

> I would say the Southeast took the initiative in terms of trying to get a formula (for funding) of some kind because we felt we were getting the least amount of money from the Department of any of the Boards, yet we had the second largest adult population. As a result of a lot of moans and groans from us, the Department began to work on this formula and if the Department hadn't been supportive of it, it wouldn't have moved anywhere, like a lot of things. But we're all involved in it and we all had a say in it, no doubt about that. One of the things about the Department of Education here is the very close relationship between the Boards and the Department in terms of moving things forward, not least of all trying to get the funding...I don't know about health and the other public bodies, but certainly as far as education's concerned, we would feel quite intimately involved recently, within the public spending survey round.

Despite the CEO's view that relations are good it is also clear that he is realistic about the importance of the DENI's support for spending budgets if they are to have any real chance of success. A second CEO interview suggests a more direct involvement of the DENI in how the money should be determined and spent:

> There's a tendency in recent years for the funds to be more and more earmarked...But I don't like the principle of earmarking funds because that reduces the management discretion in the use of the funds...Earmarking funds simply says the Department is going to determine the priorities and fund them appropriately and that is a negation of the whole concept of the public and the local authority which is really set up in principle to determine local needs and to meet those needs in the best possible way...so many different projects are now being earmarked...but there are things that if they appear to be a government initiative there's no limit to the amount of money seems to be available...the evaluation of a project at some meetings was ascertained by the lot spent, not the output in terms of children, and how their needs were being met or how community needs were being met. But try and get £20,000 that's really needed, you need to move heaven and earth.

The projects referred to were mostly attempts to solve the problems generated by high levels of economic and community disadvantage in parts of Belfast, the latest of which, Making Belfast Work, has been criticised by the Public Accounts Committee for not keeping proper budgets and receipts and being unable to account for substantial amounts of money spent ostensibly on community projects.

In the context of direct rule, the power of government ministers is substantial in the absence of normal (in Great Britain) government structures to which they could be made responsible for decisions. In real terms, however, most, as one of the CEOs put it, 'knew his place' in so far as they were sensitive to their unusual position of being responsible for the framing and administration of local education policy whilst their constituencies and accountability lay elsewhere. The position was radically altered by the appointment of an education minister originally from Northern Ireland who, in his commitment and approach, appeared to many to have a very definite view about the shape of schooling very much in line with New Right Conservative policy at the time. His impact was felt as much by civil servants in the DENI as individual Boards, one CEO commented:

> In the absence of a reasonable local government it's inevitable that that sort of thing happens. The Department more and more want to take complete control, I mean the permanent secretaries are from this province, by and large. Mawhinney upset it a little bit because he was not just a beacon for others as some of his predecessors have been. He was more uncontrollable and perhaps in fairness to him…he achieved a lot. He stirred it up and I don't agree with every thing he did but I don't think any minister has achieved as much as he has in the time he was here. A lot of what he achieved has been either Conservative government policy or his own ideas within it. But he was prepared to take on the civil servants as a politician and has been quite successful in that. Nick Scott (an earlier Consertive education minister) was a nicer man to work with but I suppose in simple terms, he knew his place and did as he was told and now and again intervened on behalf of the government as it were.

In one particular policy, however, Scott gave substantial support for what many feel to be one of the more positive and potentially far-seeing policies that had grown out of a small group of parents' attempts to turn schooling into a force for the reconciliation of sectarian distrust and violence. They believed this could be achieved by educating Catholic and Protestant children together in religiously integrated schools. The first and most prominent organisation in this movement was in fact called All Children Together (ACT). Despite government indifference and antipathy from the Churches, the first such school, Lagan College, was established under the auspices of ACT in 1981. It had to be founded as an independent school because of the DENI's refusal to subvent it and only achieved government funding in 1984 on becoming viable in the view of the Department and because of its popularity among parents. Initial reaction from the government had been to reiterate government policy that the state schools were in fact integrated and had been so since their establishment in the 1920s and 1930s and that there were plenty of empty places available in the sector. Whilst the state schools were officially non-denominational, the presence and influence of Protestant clergymen in the management of the schools made the schools unattractive to Catholics. This was also true in the wider sense of the schools' official neutrality in regard to the representation of British and Irish culture in the their ethos and practice. For Nationalists, however, the schools' detachment in practice from Irish history, cultural symbols, sports and language was perceived as consciously representative of Unionist governments' at best antipathetic policies towards their interests and cultural aspirations.

At worst, Nationalists were angry at successive governments' passivity, in the wider society, towards political and economic discrimination against them. The Catholic primary schools, in addition, occupy a special religious importance for parents and the Church as an essential part of the preparation of children for first communion. They are regarded as the most appropriate place for children to be taught in the faith as they are in other countries. Wider alienation, felt and experienced by Catholics, with Unionist political and cultural hegemony was expressed through the schools sector as the major social system where Catholics exercised power, having stayed out of the state system. Through schools, in other words, they could give proper status and representation of the Irish foundations of the curriculum in history, culture, language and sports. One CEO commented:

> Thinking of the integrated schools, he (Scott) was quite explicit in saying that the policy on integration within the education system was one that the Conservative government clearly and totally supported and he was unequivocal about that…he was an able man and nice to work with but didn't present the same problems to the senior civil servants as Mawhinney did.

The minister in this policy towards the establishment of integrated schools, reflected the liberal Protestant and Catholic view that if their children could be educated together they would find that they had much more in common and less to divide them than the respective sectarian ideologies so stridently and violently proclaimed. The policy was not without its difficulties and detractors inside government and these are recalled in an interview with Nicholas Scott about his period in Northern Ireland when he was responsible for education:

120

Lagan college, where tremendous foot dragging by the bureaucracy really (which they) gave me about bringing Lagan College into the maintained (funded) system...where I had a major fight with the DENI civil servants...but we did it.

The idea behind educating Protestant and Catholic children together has become popularly known as 'the contact thesis' (Spencer; 1987). In wider community terms, it has involved joint holidays to the United States, inter-school curricular projects for state and Catholic schools and more formally, the statutory commitment for all schools to introduce in their normal syllabuses education for mutual understanding and cultural heritage.

Curricular differences between the two systems have now disappeared with the common Northern Ireland Curriculum and the fact that Catholic primary and non-selective secondary schools now receive 100% funding for capital and recurrent costs means that they are on an equal financial footing. The significance of the latter lies in the fact that seventy years on from partition, the voluntary principle, as applied to the Catholic sector, has been formally and fully incorporated within Northern Ireland's state funded system of schooling. The main difference now would appear to be one of ethos: that in the Catholic sector teaching of all subjects is organised within a comprehensive religious atmosphere and that the state schools are *de jure* non-denominational but *de facto* Protestant and Unionist in outlook. Given the respective Catholic and Protestant teaching staff and enrolments of the two sectors it would be difficult for the schools not to reflect differences of religious ethos and culture underpinning so much of daily life in the wider society, where the degree of demographic separation created by the Troubles means that 90% of people live in areas where 90% of their neighbours are of the same religion. Whilst the schools are now outwardly the same in curriculum and funding, Darby and Dunn (1987) provide a concise summary of the significance of the social and cultural resonances and differences generated, they argue, by separate denominational schooling:

If practices within the schools are so similar, why does segregation matter? A more pertinent, but more elusive, argument is that, regardless of what goes on in the classrooms, the *fact* of separation is what matters...and is described as the social apartheid thesis, and is developed in two different ways. The first argument is that segregated schooling helps to initiate children into the conflict by emphasising and validating group differences and hostilities, instead of providing an opportunity for diminishing ignorance and suspicion...The second argument against segregation is also based on a particular view of school as institutions...It is the hidden curriculum, school values and rituals, group loyalty, peer influences, friendship patterns, which establishes a base upon which society

121

later builds a superstructure of political, demographic, recreational and social segregation. (P. 89-90)

Many people would argue that the policy on integrated education is one of the more positive outcomes of direct rule. It was further strengthened by the 1989 legislation which established Northern Ireland's version of the National Curriculum, part of which was the DENI's statutory duty to support and fund viable integrated schools. However, a significant level of ambivalence remains among parents when the level of support for the principle of integration is contrasted with its practical application when asked if they would send their children to an integrated school. Sample surveys suggest that support for the principle rarely drops below 60% and very often higher, whilst practical support drops to 30% and below (Darby and Dunn; 1987). These reactions indicate that both communities are, in practical terms, committed to separate schooling. More recently, a 1989 survey of 800 parents revealed support for integrated schooling among 67% of Catholics and 57% of Protestants with only a very small proportion against the idea (5% Catholic and 9% Protestant). The remainder thought that the government should 'leave things as they are'. A larger proportion than earlier was more in favour of practising integration: over a half would have preferred their children to be educated in a religiously integrated atmosphere (Cairns et al; 1993).

The Belfast chief executive, whilst recognising the extent to which power had gravitated towards DENI since 1972, managed successfully to create areas of policy within his own Board independently of the Department in the amalgamation of the three large Belfast colleges of further education. This has now become the Belfast Institute of Further and Higher Education and recently gained government approval and funding to go into partnership with the University of Ulster to establish the Springvale university campus in west Belfast. It will be built on the site of a former engineering factory and virtually on one of the peace lines dividing Catholics and Protestants in that part of Belfast. It would be fair to argue that the new Labour government, against the background of national and international approval and support for the recent successful outcome of negotiations to create an agreed political structure for Northern Ireland, which has become known as the Good Friday Agreement and its overwhelming approval by referendum, would have had great difficulty in turning down the proposal which had lain dormant for the previous two to three years. The interview reveals how the policy originated and was carried through despite opposition from DENI, on the reasonable ground of the long-term costs involved:

122

Well I have a particular interest in further education. The Department, everybody was opposed to it (amalgamation)…For a long time I felt that one of the problems in Belfast were the three separate boards of governors (of the FE colleges), all of whom were very capable and very able and very committed to what they were doing, all challenged with the development of their own individual colleges, almost with a total disregard for what the other two were doing. And that's proper. I thought the structure was wrong and I discussed it with the Board and some them seemed to pick it up and thought that if we could reduce the management of FE to one single management structure we would therefore present all the issues and the matters to one management board and they would solve them with a great deal more efficiency and effectiveness…And then the Department…put out this consultative document 'Signposts on Further Education…it freely referred to the concept of single institutes and amalgamations and rationalisation. And I said to them that's not bad for a department that started off totally opposed to the idea.

Another CEO pointed out the clear differences between his role and his counterpart in Great Britain in terms of their different degrees of independence of action:

…the fact that I get my funding 100% from central government means that I'm accountable through the permanent secretary in the DENI to the Public Accounts Committee. I know exactly where I stand as chief executive. If I were a Chief Education Officer in England and Wales, I would have some financial accountability to the local authority because apart from the rates support grant which would come from central government there would be a levy to the rates of the poll tax or whatever they call it now…As a strong believer in local government I would probably favour a system in this province if we could get it where I would be accountable to the five district councils that I serve…The way it is at the moment, the political scene, I serve. That political scene says to me you are accountable to the Public Accounts Committee. Now in my day-to-day work, if you're asking me how that influences my day-to-day work, we're fortunate enough in the Boards to have a fair amount of independence from the Department of Education as long as we don't run into overspends, as long as we don't work against government policy, to interpret government policy and to interpret our spend pattern as the board thinks.

The administrative and political effects of direct rule are spelt out clearly in this interview through a comparison of the interviewee's degree of autonomy in policy matters compared to his equivalent in England and Wales. The chief contrast appears to be the different bodies to which they are accountable. Whilst the interviewee above is similar to his counterpart in his relationship with the local authority, there is a significant difference between the composition and role of a Local Education Committee in England and Wales and an Education and Library Board in Northern Ireland. The most obvious one is the allocation of funds raised from local taxes and councillors elected directly on to education committees in Great Britain rather than appointed in Northern Ireland by the Secretary of State. Funding for education in Northern Ireland, as pointed out above, is not dependent on local taxes and comes wholly from DENI which imposes its own discipline and restrictions with respect to not 'running into overspends'. The degree of educational independence claimed would appear to be similarly circumscribed in terms of 'not working against government policy' when compared to the contrary interpretations of government policy that some English authorities have placed on central educational policies. These would include, for example, the retention of selection in parts of Manchester and Buckinghamshire and in the fifties and early 1960s the introduction of comprehensive schemes in Leicester and other authorities. The most important innovation introduced by a local authority in Northern Ireland has been the arrangements in Craigavon where a junior/senior high school scheme has replaced the secondary/grammar school pattern operating in the rest of the province. Selection has been postponed to 14 obviating the need for pupils to take the 11+ although they, and their parents, are clear about their status after junior high stage where they go on to either a senior secondary or grammar high school which, in academic terms, are similar to their counterparts in the rest of the selective system.

In Great Britain, power to frame and implement educational policy has, in real terms, gravitated more and more to the centre with a corresponding reduction in the responsibilities of local authorities. The National Curriculum, for example, was centrally determined and imposed as were Key stage testing and the shift from LEA based funding to schools having delegated budgets. These policies have also been applied to Northern Ireland without recourse to what are now the vestigial restraining influences of local authorities in Great Britain. In an area with such a deeply and historically embedded voluntary principle as represented by the Churches and the greater number of grammar schools, this might be expected. But as argued earlier, the influence of these voluntary bodies has been mostly to prevent change which they have thought, in a principled way, to be contrary to their constituencies' interests and in some instances their human rights. Their representatives on Boards do receive positive comments from the CEOs in for their reliability and hard work and the fact that the Boards provide an example where Catholic and Protestant clergy can work successfully in promoting their mutual interests:

124

The clerical representatives have played a very strong and very useful role in this Board (Belfast). We've had three from the Roman Catholic Church and four from the Protestant Churches. If you're looking for a quorum for a meeting you depend on the clerical representatives...they come to meetings because they have had a long-standing traditional interest in the education system. I do not know what we would do except move towards professionals running an education system if the clerics were taken out. I do not want that, they are very valuable.

Interviews with clergymen from the four main Protestant Churches suggest that they are equally positive towards the Education and Library Boards in their role as a bridge between the two communities in Northern Ireland, 'representing two communities and attempting to articulate their interests in education to each other and their traditions to each other'. Like the CEOs they thought the Boards had lost a considerable amount of power and had little influence on policy making. When asked if there were any substantial checks or balances within the Northern Ireland education system, the majority view was that any there might be are quite ineffective, especially at the top level. They saw the Churches' interest in education and their presence on local committees as quite legitimate along side the various other education lobbies. They felt, however, that whereas they exerted a strong influence at local level, this diminished at the centre of policy making. With regard to the way in which their views were taken into consideration during consultation over policy one minister commented: 'maybe the old Stormont would have listened to us a bit more than the minister'. With regard to the degree of independence enjoyed by local education committees another CEO placed a somewhat different interpretation on the Boards' and local councils' roles and the different relationship between central and local government:

Within the present political structure, I think if they were totally honest with themselves and with us they would simply establish a number of regional officers of the DENI and do the thing cleanly and honestly and take total control of the centre...when you think, what do the Boards do, they provide support services, we all provide training, we administer grants and allocate finance and things like that...When you analyse all of these things, they could be centralised or decentralised to considerable advantage. The situation you have in the province is quite unique because the DfEE across the water works with the local authorities and the education committees of the local authorities but those county councils still have major functions. What does our crowd do? They have their bins, their graves and pools, that's about the height of it.

Interviews were also held with politicians from the main political parties who generally agreed with each other about their relative lack of influence although they felt that, in some specific policies, they had been able to change a particular minister's mind. One gave an example of a minister's lack of knowledge of community level politics and the unintended effects of introducing British legislation in the context of some of the highly politicised areas of the province which would have meant Boards of Governors in many instances being dominated by Sinn Fein supporters: 'He (the minister) could not understand that decent people in most of those areas had given up and had walked away and that those who would be interested would be Sinn Fein supporters'. With regard to the power of the Education Boards in policy areas, it was felt by a Social Democratic Labour Party politician that they were still important and exercised a good deal of influence although it does not mean that they are any less politicised than other aspects of public life in Northern Ireland as one politician found to his cost:

> The Boards are very, very important. At the local level the Boards are the cause of either pouring oil on troubled waters or creating more divisiveness…at Board level the allocation of resources is very important. The merging of schools…In Belfast there are a number of schools that were on the controlled (state) side which were closed. There had to be rationalisation of Protestant schools, secondary and primary because of the demographic shift. There was a (Protestant) school about to close, a parish priest came to me, I was on the Board at the time, and said, we would buy this school from the Board and we could save a lot of money. And I was an awful lot younger and more innocent then and I went along to senior officials on the Board and said look here's this you're trying to get rid of it, this is something that the Catholic Church of all places are interested in, will you sell it? Well they went away to think about it. Next Board meeting, a proposal came forward out of the air that it would be made into a new library and youth centre and of course for the last 10 years it has been made into anything and everything rather than sell it…the Holy Family parish had to build their own. It's government money going round in circles.

The elected status of local politicians, he thought, still gives them a degree of influence in regard to their ability to bypass DENI officials:

> But councillors are elected and you get used to dealing with people in a particular way and you get used to dealing at a particular level and you scare the living day lights out of them, the officials, because you're going to go public…But as well as being elected and a representative on the Board you are also part of another organisation, the party, which ultimately can do a terrible thing which is ask a question in the House of Commons of the minister. That terrifies the

officials...the minister has to answer and they clear the decks to answer a question about so and so...And then the other MP gets up and says, if that is the case, can the minister then explain why...and you can hear the thud of bodies falling all over the place.

Throughout the period of the present Troubles the Churches have alternatively been seen as havens of stability or as part of the problem. In disadvantaged areas of Belfast particularly they provide an extra source of support:

> The Churches are very important...as a way of preserving stability in society, preserving values, preserving morals. It may be the area I represent, which is getting worse all the time. In the good parts of it, 35% of the births are to single girls. We're looking at parts of Belfast where most of the population would be under 20 and say 40% of the population would be between 9 and 19. A lot of the values have gone in this respect as well...this is actually both sides of the fence...talking to ...last night, a Presbyterian, who confirmed the same kind of thing...If you get a mortgage you get out and ...the only people who are left are the clergy, the Churches and they're up against it. There aren't enough of them. They have the schools and they can use those as sort of units attached to the Church within the area, working after hours, because the teachers all leave. You take somewhere like west Belfast, 4pm there's a slam of doors and the skidding of tyres , you try getting in to west Belfast at 8.45 a m. At the roundabout at Broadway, there are a thousand teachers trying to get round that roundabout and get in. (SDLP politician)

In another interview a Unionist MP gave a more benign view of the 'culture of officialdom' in so far as the civil servants provided a degree of stability in the context of political changes at government level and with respect to individual ministers many of whom knew little about the system and yet were making important decisions about the future of schools:

> Permanent secretaries and chief inspectors are very, very powerful people within the present education system. If they did not do it I wonder...who would actually happen. At least I would rather have (the permanent secretary) of this world than the (minister) running education...

With regard to the Churches the MP thought that, 'I do not think in this day and age the Churches should have any special power as of right...they should take their place in the queue like everybody else'. There was agreement among politicians that the lack of accountability derives from the system of direct rule and the Order-in-Council procedure which is resented by all parties. This has been compounded by the fact that ministers during their time of office have other interests and departments within the Northern Ireland Office

127

to look after as well as constituency obligations in Great Britain. One MP commented, 'most importantly they are not of the culture and do not have the background in it'. In addition, some were more interested than others, ranging from those who were merely titular heads of the DENI to those who were more interventionist with a 'mission' to carry out central government policy in the province. On recent minister, in particular, was intent on implementing government policy framed in the context of the problems of English schools, irrespective of the view of local politicians of any party. Their arguments for policies that were sensitive to the different needs and circumstances of schools in Northern Ireland were seen as part of the problem by the particular minister the Unionist MP had in mind:

> At governmental level it was decided there would be changes and you had a different problem in Northern Ireland than you had in (other) parts of the United Kingdom…especially in the south-east in the big conurbanations and I think we have got the knock-on effect here where I think things are entirely different. Teachers here are not political zealots like a lot of those that I have met around London and for that reason for somebody like (the minister) coming across with this same attitude that really teachers were not to be trusted…it must be something imposed by government.

From a Protestant view, their Chuches' power to influence education policy was much less than in the past and correctly so, it was felt, since the schools were now funded entirely by the state. There was a view that Churches of all denominations remained a significant reference point for governments in framing policy. The argument revolved around the Churches' role in preserving a bedrock of stability among some of the most troubled areas in Northern Ireland: that, in fact, the degree of unrest and conflict would have been greater without the ameliorating influence of the Churches:

> A lot of young people have identified with a culture of violence rather than religion and the Churches have a major input into schools and into education as a way of empowering young people and making them feel a part of something and that what they believe in is worthwhile.

In another aspect of policy the Protestant Churches have been successful in persuading the government to protect small state schools in border areas despite the more general push towards closure on grounds of costs and curricular coverage as well as an attempt to increase the amount of money actually reaching pupils by reducing administration costs. One SDLP politician gave an insight into the way the policy first emerged in public:

I was at a conference...and was approached by Bishop McMullen (Church of Ireland) ...and he said, 'look we have a problem in the Clogher diocese. If he (the minister) goes along the lines he's pursuing, a lot of our schools will have to close. They're small rural primary schools, symbols and beliefs that are essential to both communities. They're small secondary schools, 200-220. Now my parents are already starting to look across the border to Cavan and Monaghan (in the Republic) to send their kids of 12 to Protestant schools, but if they close these schools which are our expression of our existence as a minority along the border then I'm afraid my lot will disappear and the Church of Ireland'. So the Church, the school, the whole thing taken together provides a focus of community identity and it provides a number of emblems. (SDLP Politician)

DENI perspectives were expressed by a former permanent secretary, a senior civil servant and a former senior member of the inspectorate. All three, as might be expected, had no doubt that power to frame and operate policy lay with the minister of the day. Their role, as civil servants, lay in pointing out the practical implications of policies and suggesting, where appropriate, alternative approaches. Whilst they saw this as the proper duty of a civil servant in their advisory role, if a minister was determined on a particular policy against their advice they had to fall into line and put it into practice:

That's something that maybe as a civil servant you might fume about but I suppose being realistic and reasonable, it has to be and must necessarily be ministers that take the decision...I may not be comfortable with a decision that's made but once it's made that is how it is and I would implement it and do it. But the responsibility the person who has to stand up and be accountable for this ultimately is the minister, it isn't me, it isn't the permanent secretary...the uncomfortable point within Northern Ireland is that this defence is done by people who are not directly elected from within Northern Ireland so you get back to that point, would that have been different but that's the only speculation we could make. (Former senior inspector)

He went on to suggest that power was exercised mainly through finance and legislation and since the Boards, CCMS and other bodies were only marginally involved in both, their chief role was in the different interpretations they put on aspects of policy. In acting autonomously, however, their influence on policy was necessarily weakened because in many instances they were unable to present a collective view to the minister:

...it has always seemed to me that the chief executives don't really know if they are chief executives or chief education officers. They are professional and they see themselves as professionals but their role is really administrative rather than professional and they kind of fall between two stools. So I wouldn't put

129

them very high on the list of people influencing policy. I think the most powerful influence of all is the inspectorate. There's no doubt about that at all in my mind and it's a thoroughly good influence too. (Former permanent secretary)

With regard to the Churches he thought that, 'They influence policy in the sense that one knows what the Churches will stand for …I would say it's a fairly negative influence'. A Westminster politician who was formerly in charge of education in Northern Ireland on arriving in the DENI commented:

Your education system is a strange thing for an Englishman to come to, it was much less 'progressive' than I had been accustomed to in England. Obviously they kept the grammar schools which in part explained the very good performance of many of the better qualified children in Northern Ireland, but it still left behind a central chunk of children.

In the case of integrated education it was clear from the DENI interviews that their introduction was a Westminster driven policy. One interviewee put forward the view that:

Everybody in Westminster believes on the whole that integrated education is somehow going to solve all our problems and if ministers want to make themselves popular with their colleagues in Westminster all they have to do is to support integrated education. It was a conscious political decision that the Department should encourage integrated education.

A former Alliance party politician when asked about the groups outside DENI with the greatest influence on policy singled out the grammar school lobby and suggested that one of the reasons for its strength and the persistence of selection lay in the extent to which former pupils were often those who were centrally involved in policy decisions. 'Most of the guys who run the DENI are from that very (grammar school) lobby'. This interviewee had in fact been the chairman of the Northern Ireland Assembly's Education Committee following the creation of the Northern Ireland Assembly in 1982. Its remit was to 'shadow' the work of civil servants and comment more generally on government policy. It had the same sort of powers in terms of scrutinising policy and government departments as Select Committees with regard to questioning civil servants publicly about policy decisions on the basis of written submissions. The system of committees established under the authority of the Assembly was effective in the amount of information that they were able to gather much of which would have remained locked away in the government machine. They were also effective in providing in practical terms the only form of political scrutiny of government policy by locally elected politicians during the period of direct rule. However, the abstention of the SDLP and the ambivalence of the largest party, the official Unionist Party, meant that the Committee had much less political impact than it otherwise might have had. The most effective members were the otherwise politically opposed Alliance and Democratic Unionists with attendance records of respectively 88% and 70% contrasted with 46% for the Official Unionists (Wilford; 1987).

The chairman of the Committee reflected on his relationship with the DENI:

> On reflection I think it was a mistake to locate the DENI in Bangor ...isolated from the mainstream and government departments and inaccessible and that encouraged a total empire mentality. Cut off from the civil service, cut off from the world, and really they didn't like anybody poking into what they saw as their absolute prerogative. So in terms of influence clearly the decisions were made within the DENI and they were in my view contemptuous of outsiders, particularly politicians.

In an interview with the first director of the Council for Catholic Maintained Schools, he thought that policy-making in education was often dependent on the strength of ministerial interest. At the same time, he thought it was often made by accident or force of circumstance and was in any case largely derivative of what happened in DfEE. Northern Ireland had only rarely established original policies in education. The main one, he suggested was selection, where the grammar school lobby had always been strong added to the fact that it gained at least passive support from nearly all of those who deal with selection in the Boards and DENI who were themselves successful products of selection. After some initial difficulties with the Boards and the Department concerning the level and quality of consultation with the CCMS, and a perception that the Council might become a sixth Board competing with the other five, CCMS was now consulted on all matters that affected the Catholic sector. Policy and information is now channelled through CCMS whereas in the past it was a matter between individual Boards of Trustees and the DENI. Some insights into the background of creating CCMS were given by a senior civil servant:

> The reason CCMS was set up was supposed to address specific deficiencies in the management of maintained schools. We had 700 individual education authorities all going their separate way. There was no central direction, there was no central management, there was even no central procedures for doing anything. If we wanted to consult on a very small issue the Department ...had to write round all 700 of them and there was no clear consensus on the maintained side at all. There was no continuity of employment if a teacher charged from school to school. It was really a very unsatisfactory system all round.

131

CCMS now consults and negotiates on behalf of trustees with DENI and its relationship with government and the Boards has now stabilised. The first director of CCMS did lay great stress on the spiritual dimension of the Council's role:

> In such a changing climate I see the Council's function as guarding against the current trend of growing materialism in educational thinking and positively striving to ensure the preservation of that which is good in the long term interest of the whole person of the child and consequently of both Church and society.

In summary, a number of themes concerning the exercise of power and equity in relation to the framing and implementation of educational policy emerge from the views of those who were interviewed. It is evident that direct rule gives little scope for publicly accountable scrutiny available elsewhere in the United Kingdom. In recognition of this form of 'democratic deficit' the government has recently introduced a Select Committee to partially fill this gap. To a large extent direct rule of Northern Ireland's affairs from Westminster has given rise within the province to the politics of influence groups as particular lobbies have either attempted to hold on to what they have or to change the system. The grammar schools clearly emerge as a powerful and sucessful lobby as judged by the virtually unchallenged retention of selective schooling based in turn on the schools' popularity and the esteem in which they are held. Parents, in other words, are keenly aware of the added value that the schools give and the sort of academic and social start that their children receive from a grammar school education. They also appreciate, for instance, the direct vocational pay-off the schools confer with regard to access to higher education and from there to a wide range of professions. Just as importantly in today's 'flexible' employment market the schools open the way to occupations which are relatively secure. Politicians of both parties who have been in power over the last 26 years have recognised this populist support for the schools.

In the case of the Conservatives, they have been more than happy to support the schools and on occasion have held them up as an example of the benefits of grammar schools in their attempts to re-introduce selection in England and Wales. The excellence of the schools in attaining the best A level results in the United Kingdom is most often quoted as evidence that selection could similarly raise standards in what they consider to be largely failing English comprehensive schools. The downside of the equation, that the Northern Ireland selective system also produces the greatest number of pupils leaving with poor or no qualifications is not so often given, although this has been more recently targeted by both parties through the RSSI and the recently announced School Improvement Programme. Whilst schools will always reflect wider patterns of inequality and disadvantage with regard to the skills and knowledge that pupils from different backgrounds bring to school, politicians seem to ignore the fact that selection exacerbates this inequity further. Open enrolment within a selective system has meant, for example, that grammar schools have now extended the academic creaming effect of selection to cover upwards of 40% of the age group. This has led to both structural insecurity in the secondary sector in terms of enrolments, staffing and also in relation to their 'mission'. Are they to be 11-16 schools feeding into the 11-18 grammars? If this is the case then they should be allowed an equal spread of ability on intake otherwise they will forever be disadvantaged in competing with the grammar schools. One politician interviewee felt that the grammar schools had influenced educational policy far in excess of their presence in the overall system:

> The existence of separate voluntary grammar schools clearly has (an impact) because this has been the factor that decides just about everything important in Northern Ireland...at university level, through the secondary schools down to the primary schools through the 11+. Socially they're very powerful, politically they've been powerful and financially they've been powerful. They used that power to serve their own interests, but yes, it was much more negative in that it kept a very divisive secondary system going for so long...

The segregated structure of the system is also a realisation by politicians of the influence of the Churches as representative of their respective communities' interests in maintaining their separate cultural and religious identities through schooling. For Catholics, their schools are also perceived as a means, in the past, of combating discrimination and, at present, of attaining equality in employment and in the wider representation of Nationalist culture. One of the politicians commented: 'I think it's probably stronger on the Catholic side because of the whole history politically and sociologically of the Catholic community. In a sense the importance of the education system as they would see it for their own community'. The Protestant Churches have been less influential because, unlike the Catholic Church, they do not own the schools although they still retain rights of membership on individual Boards of Governors from the 1930 Act. Their current argument for a Transferors' Representative Council to give official recognition of a Protestant ethos in the state school, is a recognition of their diminished position in comparison they claim to the preferential treatment of the Catholic Authorities through their membership of the CCMS. They also refer to the special treatment of the integrated sector in the establishment of the Northern Ireland Council for Integrated Education (NICIE), funded by DENI, which now administers the affairs of the integrated school sector and advises on policy.

The integrated schools lobby has been successful in persuading Westminster politicians that in educating Catholic and Protestant pupils together they can begin to understand and appreciate that they share a great deal in their different 'histories' as opposed to the street-based sectarian ideologies of suspicion and mistrust they grow up with and which have been a major cause of conflict over the last thirty years of the current Troubles. Whilst political support has built on a movement that originated with parents in Northern Ireland, the fact of DENI's statutory support for integration is part of a wider pattern of Westminster generated policies designed to establish some degree of cross-community consensus. It is a moot point as to whether or not integrated schools would have grown to their current numbers in the absence of direct rule given the opposition of the Catholic Church in particular and the Protestant Churches' ambivalence. One Catholic politician commented: 'I know the way I would have been treated by the Catholic Church because of my support for integrated education. I was *persona non grata* with my local priests'. The presence of selection has also helped the growth of integration to some extent by giving parents an alternative to the non-selective secondary school in the event of their child failing' the test and being unable to obtain a grammar school place. The schools are perceived by parents as being somewhere between the grammar and secondary school academically and, just as importantly, from a parental viewpoint their more attractive social mix of pupils.

The priority given to integrated schooling can be gauged from an observation of a senior DENI official:

> We have to sponsor the creation of school places even in an area where there are already surplus places, but these are school places of a particular sort and they are in response to particular parental demand. So even if there are empty places in other schools, if there is a demand for integrated education places, that demand has got the same right to be met as demands from other schools.

In an interview with a Northern Ireland journalist specialising in education, the success of integration, he suggested, was just as importantly based on the strength of purpose of the parents. In the context of the government policy of parental choice and wider preferences for market forces as the determining factor in schooling their campaign for integrating schooling and especially its potential for community understanding and reconciliation

134

made it difficult for the DENI to resist and culminated in the movement gaining official support and funding:

> Parents can be active…There's a decision to close a school and parents become active and they run a campaign and sometimes they succeed, more usually they don't. The group then disappears. The schools close, the children move to another school. The obvious exception is parents campaigning for integrated education because theirs has been…more constructive. They've a long-term objective and some of them have stuck with that for quite a few years and learned a lot and in the process learned a lot on the political process; learned how to organise and how to raise finance, learned how to keep everyone happy and achieve their objectives.

In discussing the role of DENI in framing policy and its more general oversight of the education system he put it in a surprisingly positive light:

> I'm saying the broad structure (of policy) comes from the top, but precise form I think is greatly influenced by what comes from the bottom…I get the feeling that there is much more real consultation in Northern Ireland with those who are in the classroom than there is in Britain. And it's partly because a number of the civil servants and ministers in Northern Ireland are keenly aware of their position and are actually quite keen to do something about it. What it means is that in Northern Ireland ministers and civil servants, if they wish to abuse power greatly they could. We haven't abused power up to now and they've gone out of their way to try and consult. In Britain, if you speak to Local Education Authorities or to teacher unions or to any of the groups involved outside of the favoured few they will tell you that they are entirely ignored.

The deep-rooted political and cultural differences which are outwardly expressed in a largely segregated schooling system means that the majority of children will attend schools with others of the same religion and cultural outlook. The former director of CCMS estimated that integrated schools would grow such that: 'There would be sufficient support for an integrated school in virtually every sizeable town in Northern Ireland, I am not sure I would see it growing much beyond that'. However, for most parents the legitimacy of the current segregated pattern of schooling is unquestioned. Their reasons are not wholly based on religious or cultural identity, the absence of any significant number of independent schools, for instance, apart from a few religious foundations, is an indication of parents' confidence in state-funded schools of either religious ethos. The situation is strongly contrasted with areas of England where there has been growth in private provision commensurate with parents' declining confidence in state schools. This has been partly driven by the Conservative government's attitudes to state education during the 1980s and

1990s which focused, they claimed, on teachers' unquestioning acceptance of unsuitable and intellectually debilitating 'progressive' teaching methods. These, it was claimed, gave children's needs primacy in the organisation of learning rather than the intellectual demands of the traditional academic subjects. Such child-centred teaching had been responsible, in the view of the influential educational right, for a drop in educational standards nationally, poor attitudes to the needs of the economy and, more pejoratively, rising levels of anti-social behaviour. 'Progressive' teaching methods have been adopted in the province but not to the same extent as in England and classroom teaching reflects a more conservative approach to education in general. The same is true in the retention of selection for which there is no overwhelming pressure from parents to change to a non-selective system of post-primary education. More sceptically, the present high levels of access to grammar schools for middle class and ambitious working class parents also contributes to the current degree of support for selection.

The prospect of a return to local control of education and other parts of government as a result of current political developments or what has become known as the 'Good Friday Agreement' will place the system's problems back in the hands of Northern Ireland politicians. This has been one of the positive outcomes stressed by those in favour of the Agreement and it would render policy making more publicly visible and accountable than it ever could be during the period of direct rule given the fact that policy has been framed by politicians whose constituencies are in Great Britain. Several pressing problems will remain:

- how to improve the expectations and qualifications of pupils from disadvantaged areas and the status of schools in the secondary sector;

- to consider seriously the extension of the arrangements in the Craigavon where selection is postponed to 14 and based on normal academic progress as opposed to a singular 'high-stakes' test which distorts parts of the primary curriculum; and

- to consider the particular circumstances and strengths and weaknesses of the Northern Ireland system in framing policy rather than creating a mirror image of arrangements in England and Wales.

In this last respect, the referendum on the Good Friday Agreement has produced a substantial majority in its favour (71% said yes) giving a mandate for local politicians to establish in the first instance an Assembly through which they will 'shadow' the work of Westminster MPs currently in charge. If the Assembly works successfully, power will be transferred formally in February 1999 which will represent the first opportunity since 1972, and briefly in 1974, for local politicians to exercise power in the framing and implementation of policy in education and other areas of government. A local administration will remove the feeling expressed by many of being 'governed from afar' and will place the responsibility for funding and its distribution in the hands of Northern Ireland politicians. Whether it changes what some researchers have labelled the 'culture of officialdom' as the context of policy-making and decisions about schooling remains to be seen. Much will depend on the degree of political consensus that can be achieved in the Assembly, otherwise civil servants, as they have done during the period of direct rule, will again 'pick up the pieces'. In this respect, the recent election of members to the Northern Ireland Assembly augurs well for the future administration of the provinces affairs: 75% of those elected support the Agreement and have pledged to work positively within the new Assembly. At the first meeting of the Assembly the leader of the Unionist party and a senior SDLP politician were elected on a joint ticket by the members as, respectively, First and Deputy First Minister of the Assembly. Even a year ago such co-operation would have been inconceivable and is an indication of how radically the politics of Northern Ireland are being re-aligned.

References

Aunger E., (1975) Religion and Occupational Class in Northern Ireland, *Economic and Social Review*, 7(1) P.1-18.

Akenson D., (1973) *Education and Enmity*, London, Harper and Row.

Altusser L., (1972) Ideology and Ideological State Apparatuses, in Cosin, B., Dale, I., R., Esland, G.,M., and Swift, D., F., (eds) *School and Society*, London, Routledge and Kegan Paul.

Astin Report (1979) Report of the Working Party on the Management of Schools in Northern Ireland, Belfast, HMSO.

Beckett J., C., (1966) *The Making of Modern Ireland*, London, Faber.

Belfast Health Commisioners Report (1908), Belfast, Public Records Office for Northern Ireland.

Bell D., (1972) On Meritocracy and Equality, *The Public Interest*, 29 (Fall).

Breen R., and Gudgin G., (1996) *An Evaluation of the Ration of Unemployment as an Indicator of Fair Employment*, Report No 4, Belfast, Central Community Relations Unit.

Bourdieu P., (1988) *Language and Symbolic Power*, Cambridge, Polity Press.

Bourdieu P., and Passeron J-C., (1990) *Reproduction*, London, Sage.

Bowles S., and Gintis H., (1976) *Schooling in Capitlaist America*, London, Routledge Kegan and Paul.

Cairns E., Dunn S., and Giles M., (1993) Surveys of Integrated Education in Northern Ireland: A Review, in Osborne R., D., Cormack R., J., and Gallagher A., M., *After the Reforms: Education and Policy in Northern Ireland*, Aldershot, Avebury Press.

Cameron Report (1969) *Disturbances in Northern Ireland*, Report of the Commission Appointed by the Governor of Northern Ireland. Belfast, HMSO Cmd. 532.

Caul R., L., and Harbison, J., I., (1989) The Curriculum in Small Schools in Northern Ireland and Scotland, *Irish Education Studies*, 8:2 p.117-137.

Central Statistical Office (1994) *Regional Trends 29*, London, HMSO

Cathcart H., R., (1984) *The Most Troublsome Region: The BBC in Northern Ireland*, Belfast, Blackstaff Press.

Cathcart H., R., (1990) The Politics of No Change, in Caul, *Schools under Scrutiny*, London, Macmillan.

Caul R., L., (1994) *School Effectiveness in Northern Ireland*, Belfast, Standing Commission for Human Rights.

Commission for Social Justice; 1994. London, Vintage.

Coolahan, J., (1981), *Irish Education: Its History and Structure*, Dublin, Institute of Public Administration.

Cormack R., J., Gallagher A., M., and Osborne R., D., (1991) *Educational Affiliation and Educational Attainment in Northern Ireland: The financing of Schools in Northern Ireland*, Annex E, 16th Report of the Standing Advisory Commission for Human Rights, house of Commons, Paper 488, London, HMSO.

Daly P., (1987) School Effectiveness and Pupils' Examination Performance in Northern Ireland in R., D., Cormack R., J., and Miller R., L., *Education and Policy in Northern Ireland*, Belfast, Policy Research Institute.

Daly P., (1991) How Large are School Effects in Northern Ireland? *School Effectiveness and School Improvement*, 2 (4) P. 305-323.

Darby J., and Dunn S., Segregated Schooling: The Research Evidence, in Osborne R., D., Cormack R., J., and Miller R., L., *Education and Policy in Northern Ireland*, Belfast, Policy Research Institute.

Department of Education for Northern Ireland (1977) *Report of the Working Party on Alternative Transfer Arrangements*, Belfast, HMSO.

Department of Education for Northern Ireland (1994) *Learning for Life*, Belfast, HMSO.

Department of Education for Northern Ireland (1996) *Strategic Plan for Education*, Belfast, HMSO.

Department of Education for Northern Ireland (1996) *Transfer Procedure Results*, 1989/90-1995/96, Statistical Bulletin, SB1/96.

Department of Education for Northern Ireland (1996) Statistical Bulletin, *Free School Meals and Low Achievement*, Statistical Bulletin, SB2/96.

Department of Education for Northern Ireland, (1997) *An Initial Analysis of The Impact of Formula Funding and Local Management of Schools*, Research briefing: RB 4/97, Statistics Branch, Bangor.

Department of Education for Northern Ireland (1997) Statistical Bulletin, *Qualifications of Norhtern Ireland School Leavers* 1993-94 and 1994 - 95.

Department of Education for Northern Ireland (1998), *School Improvement*, Belfast, HMSO.

Douglas, J., W., B., (1964) *The Home and the School*, London, MacGibbon and McKee.

Farren, S., (1995) *The Politics of Irish Education, 1920-1960*, Belfast, Queen's University, Institute of Irish Studies.

Finegold D., (1993) Breaking out of the Low-skill Equilibrium, in *Briefings*; National Commission on Education, London, Hamlyn.

Fiske R., (1985) *In time of War*, Paladin, London.

Foster R., (1989) *Modern Ireland 1600-1972*, London, Penguin.

Fraser S., (1997) Introduction to the Bell Curve Wars, in Halsey A., H., Lauder H., Brown P., and Stuart Wells A., *Education, Culture, Economy, Society*, Oxford, Oxford University Press.

Gallagher A., M.,(1988) *Transfer Pupils at Sixteen*, Report No 4, Belfast, NICER.

Gallagher, A., M., (1993a) Community Relations, Equality and Education, in Osborne Cormack R., J., and Gallagher A., M., *After the Reforms: Education and Policy in Northern Ireland*, Aldershot, Avebury Press.

Gallagher, A., (1993b) *Small Rural Primary Schools: A Research Review*, Cookstown, Rural Development Council.

Gallagher A., M., McEwen A., and Knipe D., (1995) *Girls and A level Science*, Belfast, Equal Opportunities Commission.

Gallagher, A., M., (1996) U*nderachievement in Northern Ireland*, Submission to the N. I. Affairs Committee, HOC Paper 79, November 1996, London, HMSO.

Gallagher A., M., Shuttleworth I., and Gray C., (1997) *Educational Achievement in Northern Ireland: Patterns and Prospects*, Belfast, Northern Ireland Economic Council.

Galton M., and Patrick H., (1990) *Curriculum Provision in the Small Primary School*, London, Routledge.

Goldthorpe J., H., (1968-69) *The Affluent Worker in the Class Structure*, (3 vols.) Cambridge, Cambridge University Press.

Green A., and Steadman H., (1993) *Educational Provision, Educational Attainment and the Needs of Industry: A Review of Research for Germany, France, Japan, the USA*, Report Series No 5. London, National Institute of Economic and Social Research.

Greer J., and Long J., (1989) Catholic and Protestant Pupils' Religious Values, *Education North* 1:2.

Halsey A., H., Heath A., F., and Ridge J., M., (1980) *Origins and Destinations*, Oxford, Oxford University Press.

Hadow Report, (1926) *Report of the Consultative Commitee of the Board of Education on The Education of the Adolescent.*

Halsey A., H., (1993) Opening Wide the Doors of Higher Education, in *Briefings*; National Commission on Education, London, Hamlyn.

Halsey A., H., Lauder H., Brown P. and Stuart Wells A. (1997) *Education, Culture, Economy, Society*, Oxford, Oxford University Press.

Howieson C. (1993) Parity of Academic and Vocational Awards: the Experience of modularisation in Scotland, *European Journal of Education*, (28) 2, P 177-187.

Jencks C., (1972) *Inequality: A re-assessment of the Effects of Family and School in America*, New York, Basic Books.

Jowell R., Witherspoon S., and Brook L., (1990) *British Social Attitudes: The 7th Report*, London, Gower.

Kamin L., J., (1974) *The Science and Politics of IQ*, New York, Wiley.

Kellaghan T., and Greaney B., J., (1993) *The Education and Development of Students Following Participation in a Pre-School Programme in a Disadvantaged Area of Dublin*, Bernard van Leer Foundation Studies and Evaluation, Paper No. 12.

Kennedy D., (1971) Catholic Education in Northern Ireland, in *Aspects of Catholic Education*, Belfast, St Mary's College of Education.

Leckey J., McEwen A., Paul J., A., and Salters M., G., (1993) *An Investigation of Public Policy with Respect to Education in Northern Ireland*, Graduate School of Education, Queen's University Belfast.

141

Livingstone J., (1987) Equality of opportunity in Education in Northern Ireland, in Osborne R., D., Cormack R., J., and Miller R., L., *Education and Policies in N.Ireland*.

Lyons F., S., L., (1971) *Ireland Since the Famine*, London, Fontana.

McCavera P., (1997) *Church/State Relationships and Roman Catholic Schools in Northern Ireland 1922-1996*, Unpublished PhD Thesis, Belfast, Graduate School of Education, Queen's University.

McGill P., (1996a) *Targeting Social Needs*, Belfast, Northern Ireland Council for Voluntary Action.

McGill P., (1996b) *Under-achievement in Northern Ireland*, Submission to the Northern Ireland Affairs Committee, HOC Paper 79, November 1996, London, HMSO.

McGill P., (1997) *Education and Training*, Belfast, Standing Advisory Commission on Human Rights, London, HMSO.

McKelvey H., (1993) The Education Reforms in Northern Ireland: The Transferors' Perspective, in Osborne R., D., Cormack R., J., and Gallagher A., M., 1993 (eds), *After the Reforms: Education and Policy in Northern Ireland*, Aldershot, Avebury Press.

McKeown P., (1993) The Introduction of Formula Funding and Local Management of Schools, in Northern Ireland in Osborne R., Cormack R., J., and Gallagher A., M., *After the Reforms: Education and Policy in Northen Ireland*, Aldershot, Avebury Press.

McKeown P,. Byrne G., and Barnett R. (1996) *An Initial Analysis of The Impact of Formula Funding and Local Management of Schools*, Jordanstown, School of Public Policy, University of Ulster.

McKeown P., and Byrne G., (1998) Schooling, the Churches and the State in Northern Ireland: A Continuing Tension?, in *Research Paperss in Education*.

Mortimore P., Sammons P., Stoll L., Lewis D., and Ecob R., (1988) *School Matters: The Junior Years*, Wells, Open Books.

Sammons P., Hillman J., and Mortimer P., (1995) *Key Characteristics of Effective Schools*, London University, Institute of Education.

Murray D., (1993) Science and Funding in Northern Ireland Grammar Schools, in Osborne R., D., Cormack R., J., and Gallagher A., M., (eds), *After the Reforms: Education and Policy in Northern Ireland*, Aldershot, Avebury Press.

Murray D., and Darby J., (1980) *The Vocational Aspirations and Expectations of School Leavers in Londonderry and Strabane*, Fair Employment Agency, Research Paper 6, Belfast, FEA.

National Commission on Education, (1993), *Learning to Succeed*, London, Heinemann.

Northern Ireland Economic Council (1995*), Reforming the Educational System in Northern Ireland*, Belfast.

Northern Ireland Economic Council (1997*), Educational Achievement in Northern Ireland: Patterns and Prospects*, Paper No. 4, Belfast.

142

O'Boyle, M., (1993) Rhetoric and Reality in Northern Ireland's Catholic Secondary Schools, in Osborne R., D., Cormack R., J., and Gallagher A., M., (eds), *After the Reforms: Education and Policy in Northern Ireland*, Aldershot, Avebury Press.

O'Dowd L., Rolston W., and Tomlinson M., (1980) *Northern Ireland: Between Civil Rights and Civil War,* London, CSE Books.

Osborne R., D. Cormack R., J., and Miller R., L., (1987) *Education and Policy in Northern Ireland*, Belfast, Policy Research Institute.

Pahl R., (1985) *Divisions of Labour*, Cambridge, Blackwell.

Powis Report (1870) *Royal Commission of Inquiry into Primary Education* (Ireland) F, section 3, (Belfast District), H.C.1870.

Rutter M., Maughan B., Mortimore P., amd Ouston J., (1979) *Fifteen Thousand Hours*: *Secondary Schools and their Effects on Children*, London, Open Books.

Spencer A., E., C., W., (1987) Arguments for an Integrated School System, in Osborne R., D. Cormack R., J., and Miller R., L., (1987) *Education and Policy in Northern Ireland*, Belfast, Policy Research Institute.

Schiff M., and Lewontin R., (1986) *Education and Class: The Irrelevance of IQ and Genetic Studies*, Oxford, Oxford University Press.

Sharp C., and Kendall L., (1996*) Completion of A level andGNVQ Courses in Schools: a Research Study*, London, SCAA.

Spens Report (1938) *Report of the Consultative Committee of the Board of Education on Secondary Education with special reference to Grammar Schools and Technical High Schools.*

Sutherland A., (1993) The Transfer Reformed? in Osborne R., D., Cormack R., J., and Gallagher A., M., (eds), *After the Reforms: Education and Policy in Northern Ireland*, Aldershot, Avebury Press.

Thomas S., and Mortimore P., (1994) Report on Value Added Analysis of 1993 GCSE Examination results in Lancashire. (In press*) Research Papers in Education.*

Walford G. (1992) Selection for Secondary Schooling in *Briefings*; National Commission on Education, London, Hamlyn.

Wilford R. (1987) The Education Committee of the Northern Ireland Assembly, in Osborne in R., D. Cormack R., J., and Miller R., L., *Education and Policy in Northern Ireland*, Belfast, Policy Research Institute.

Wilms J., D., and McPherson A., (1997) Equalisation and Improvement: Some Effects of Comprehensive Reorganisation in Scotland, in Halsey A., H., Lauder H., Brown P., and Stuart Wells A., *Education, Culture, Economy, Society*, Oxford, Oxford University Press.

Willis P., (1977) *Learning to Labour: How Working Class Kids get Working class Jobs*, London, Saxon House.

Wilson J., A., (1985) *Secondary School Organisation and Pupil Progress*, Belfast, NICER.

Wilson J., A., (1987) Selection for Secondary Education, in Osborne R., D., Cormack R., J., and Miller R., L., *Education and Policy in Northern Ireland*, Belfast, Policy Research Institute. Wilson J., A., and Gardiner T., (1982) *Progress at 16*, Belfast, NICER.

Whyte J., (1990) *Interpreting Northern Ireland*, Oxford, Clarendon Press.

Index

146